formatio

TRADITION. EXPERIENCE.
TRANSFORMATION.

Formatio books from InterVarsity Press follow the rich tradition of the church in the journey of spiritual formation. These books are not merely about being informed, but about being transformed by Christ and conformed to his image. Formatio stands in InterVarsity Press's evangelical publishing tradition by integrating God's Word with spiritual practice and by prompting readers to move from inward change to outward witness. InterVarsity Press uses the chambered nautilus for Formatio, a symbol of spiritual formation because of its continual spiral journey outward as it moves from its center. We believe that each of us is made with a deep desire to be in God's presence. Formatio books help us to fulfill our deepest desires and to become our true selves in light of God's grace.

Also by James Bryan Smith

Embracing the Love of God

Rich Mullins: An Arrow Pointing to Heaven

Room of Marvels

A Spiritual Formation Workbook (with Richard J. Foster)

The Good and Beautiful God

The Good and Beautiful Life

The Good and Beautiful Community

The Kingdom and the Cross

JAMES BRYAN SMITH

HIDDEN IN CHRIST

LIVING AS GOD'S BELOVED

IVP Books

An imprint of InterVarsity Press
Downers Grove, Illinois

InterVarsity Press
P.O. Box 1400, Downers Grove, IL 60515-1426
World Wide Web: www.ivpress.com
Email: email@ivpress.com

*InterVarsity Press® is the book-publishing division of InterVarsity Christian Fellowship/USA®, a
movement of students and faculty active on campus at hundreds of universities, colleges and
schools of nursing in the United States of America, and a member movement of the International
Fellowship of Evangelical Students. For information about local and regional activities, write
Public Relations Dept., InterVarsity Christian Fellowship/USA, 6400 Schroeder Rd., P.O. Box
7895, Madison, WI 53707-7895, or visit the IVCF website at www.intervarsity.org.*

All Scripture quotations, unless otherwise indicated, are taken from THE HOLY BIBLE, NEW
INTERNATIONAL VERSION®, NIV® *Copyright © 1973, 1978, 1984, 2011 by Biblica, Inc.™
Used by permission. All rights reserved worldwide.*

*While all stories in this book are true, some names and identifying information in this book have
been changed to protect the privacy of the individuals involved.*

Cover design: Cindy Kiple
Interior design: Beth Hagenberg
Images: bird's nest: © Mayumi Terao/iStockphoto
  chick: © George Clerk/iStockphoto
  robin's nest: © 2009 Laurie Rubin Photography/Getty Images

ISBN 978-0-8308-3581-2

Printed in the United States of America ∞

Library of Congress Cataloging-in-Publication Data
Smith, James Bryan.
 Hidden in Christ : living as God's beloved / James Bryan Smith.
    pages cm
 Includes bibliographical references.
 ISBN 978-0-8308-3575-1 (alk. paper)
 1. Bible. N.T. Colossians—Devotional use. I. Title.
 BS2765.54.S65 2013
 242'.5—dc23

                                                          2013006893

| P | 16 | 15 | 14 | 13 | 12 | 11 | 10 | 9 | 8 | 7 | 6 | 5 | 4 | 3 | 2 | 1 |
| Y | 26 | 25 | 24 | 23 | 22 | 21 | 20 | 19 | 18 | 17 | 16 | 15 | 14 | 13 | | |

To my beautiful and brilliant wife, Meghan,

who guided and nurtured this book from start to finish.

CONTENTS

Acknowledgments.   9

Introduction.   11

1 Raised   19

2 With   25

3 Seated   31

4 Set   36

5 Hidden.   42

6 Life.   48

7 Revealed   54

8 You.   60

9 Mortify   66

10 Bodies   72

11 Desires.   77

12 Wrath   83

13 Walk.   89

14 Once   95

15 Mouth   101

16 Clothes 107

17 Knowledge 113

18 All 119

19 Chosen 125

20 Beloved 131

21 Bear 137

22 Forgive 143

23 Love 149

24 Peace 155

25 Thankful 161

26 Word 167

27 Teach 173

28 Sing 179

29 Whatever 185

30 Name 191

Group Discussion Guide 197

Notes 212

ACKNOWLEDGMENTS

I would like to thank my wife, Meghan, who had a vision for this book before I began. Her enthusiasm was contagious. She also read each chapter carefully and gave excellent feedback for each one.

I would also like to thank the people of Chapel Hill United Methodist Church in Wichita, who shared their insights into Colossians 3 over the past few years. Many of them found their way into this book.

Many thanks to my father-in-law, Emil Johnson, who proofread the final edition of this book—and thanks to his grammar teachers who taught him well.

Finally, I would like to thank InterVarsity Press, particularly Cindy Bunch and Jeff Crosby, who are the very best at what they do.

INTRODUCTION

*Sanctify them by the truth; your **word** is truth.*

JOHN 17:17

Colossians 3 has changed my life.

In 2002, I began memorizing Colossians 3:1-17. When you memorize a passage rather than a random verse here or there, your mind is filled with an entire system of thought, not merely an idea. Colossians 3 is a very rich passage, comprising a complete picture of our life in Christ, so it made an ideal choice to memorize.

It takes me a while to memorize a passage. I printed a few verses on a note card and carried it with me everywhere I went. I said it over and over in the morning, and throughout the day. Each night I fell asleep reciting as many verses as I could. In about a month or two I had it memorized. I continued to recite it as often as I could each day, and soon the ideas and images in the passage began to permeate my thoughts. Each day, I found a new application for some part of the passage.

A few years later I gathered a group of twenty-five people to field-test a curriculum I was creating, called the Apprentice series, to teach us how to develop Christlikeness. Knowing how powerful memorizing this passage had been for me, I asked everyone in the class to do the same. No one objected, though a few people told me initially they were certain they could not do it. I told them they could if they broke it down, verse by verse. After a month or so everyone in the class could recite Colossians 3:1-17. Over the next six months we went through the material and the exercises found in the series. In nearly every class session someone would make a reference to Colossians 3. They would say things like, "The other day I was thinking about how my life in Christ has changed, and I thought about that image of changing clothes in Colossians 3:12, about how I have taken off things like anger and put on things like compassion."

Over the next four years I would ask each new group who went through the curriculum to memorize this text. All in all, over a hundred people went through the curriculum and memorized Colossians 3, and each of them shared some new insight into the passage I had never seen before. Now, ten years later, this passage is even more fascinating for me than when I began.

One of the things you notice when you memorize a passage

is that single words stand out. In the classes we found ourselves saying, "Why does Paul say Jesus is *seated* at the right hand of God in verse 1? Does that word matter? It must, because Paul never wasted words. So, what does it mean? What does it mean in my life?"

Jesus is called the Logos in the first chapter of John's Gospel. *Logos* is the Greek word for "Word." John is telling us that Jesus is the Word of God who became flesh. One day it hit me: just as the Word became flesh in Jesus, so also our flesh becomes a word. The words in Colossians 3 have become enfleshed in my life.

Words are powerful. We are shaped by words. Words contain ideas, and they shape the way we see God, ourselves and all of reality. Single words from Colossians 3 began to bounce around in my mind, forming a new understanding of the gospel, a new awareness of who I am, and who my brothers and sisters in Christ are. I began to love the words in this passage:

- raised
- hidden
- wrath
- knowledge
- affections
- peace
- gratitude
- name

As I probed into these single words, they began to yield a deeper understanding of what it means to be an apprentice of Jesus. I found them to be a kind of corrective to many of my false ideas.

Examining the word *hidden*, for example, opened up a whole new understanding of our life in Christ. I knew from Romans 6 that those of us who have been baptized into Christ have died, were crucified with Jesus and raised with him. But in Colossians 3:3 Paul tells us that this new life in Christ is hidden with Christ in God. I had no idea what this mystery meant, but as I began to delve deeper into this word (and parallel passages) a new understanding of what it means to have my life hidden in Christ emerged, and with it a deeper gratitude to God and a more solid confidence in Jesus than ever before.

My aim in this book is to take you on this journey with me. I tried, in each of the thirty chapters, to bring out the rich insights each word had provided for me. The goal here was not to excavate some scholarly insights, but to bring forth the main truth of the word or phrase in such a way that you, the reader, will find encouragement, refreshment and enthusiasm. Paul wrote his letter to the Colossians not to give them an academic treatise on Christian theology but to tell his readers a story—the greatest story the world has ever heard. It is a story about love, self-sacrifice, new life, victory over evil, transformation, compassion, forgiveness and glory. It is the story of the extravagant love of the Trinity, who engaged in a divine conspiracy to redeem, reconcile, forgive, heal and draw all people into an intimate relationship of love.

The only way to tell a story is to use words.

How to Use This Book

The chapters in this book are short in length, making it ideal to use as a daily devotional. Since there are thirty chapters, it could be used for a one-month introduction to the hidden life in Christ. Or you may find that covering one text a day doesn't allow enough reflection time. Feel free to find the pace that is most grace-filled for you.

Each brief chapter focuses on some very deep truths from Scripture. For those who have read and practiced the exercises in the Apprentice series, this book will be a helpful encouragement for the sacred journey. Those who are unfamiliar with the Apprentice series should find this book an easy entry point into a deeper life with Christ.

Every chapter contains an exercise or practice ("Living into the Truth"), as well as a summation of the main point of the chapter ("Affirmation") and a written prayer ("Prayer") that is designed to move you deeper into the truths of the word. In addition, each chapter concludes with a few reflection questions that can be used either by individuals or in a group discussion. Thus, this book can be used privately or as part of a small group.

The best way to get the most out of this book is to

1. read the chapter

2. engage in the daily/weekly exercise

3. repeat the summative affirmation throughout the day/week

4. answer the questions using a journal

5. meet with a fellow Christ-follower or small group to discuss it together

As you go along, I encourage you also to take on the challenge of memorizing Colossians 3. It will transform your mind and heart.

May God, through the Holy Spirit, take these words and fill them with life and energy, reaching into your soul, through your mind and down into your heart, giving you joy and encouragement in your sacred journey.

James Bryan Smith

Since, then, you have been raised with Christ, set your hearts on things above, where Christ is, seated at the right hand of God. Set your minds on things above, not on earthly things. For you died, and your life is now hidden with Christ in God. When Christ, who is your life, appears, then you also will appear with him in glory.

Put to death, therefore, whatever belongs to your earthly nature: sexual immorality, impurity, lust, evil desires and greed, which is idolatry. Because of these, the wrath of God is coming. You used to walk in these ways, in the life you once lived. But now you must also rid yourselves of all such things as these: anger, rage, malice, slander, and filthy language from your lips. Do not lie to each other, since you have taken off your old self with its practices and have put on the new self, which is being renewed in knowledge in the image of its Creator. Here there is no Gentile or Jew, circumcised or uncircumcised, barbarian, Scythian, slave or free, but Christ is all, and is in all.

Therefore, as God's chosen people, holy and dearly loved, clothe yourselves with compassion, kindness, humility, gentleness and patience. Bear with each other and forgive one another if any of you has a grievance against someone. Forgive as the Lord forgave you. And over all these virtues put on love, which binds them all together in perfect unity.

Let the peace of Christ rule in your hearts, since as members of one body you were called to peace. And be thankful. Let the message of Christ dwell among you richly as you teach and admonish one another with all wisdom through psalms, hymns, and songs from the Spirit, singing to God with gratitude in your hearts. And whatever you do, whether in word or deed, do it all in the name of the Lord Jesus, giving thanks to God the Father through him.

—*Colossians 3:1-17*

1

RAISED

*Since, then, you have been **raised** with Christ . . .*

COLOSSIANS 3:1

Last year, I got a phone call you never want to receive. A friend called to tell me that a good, long-time friend had died. Sheryl and I went to college together and worked together, and she and her husband, Doug, had been some of our closest friends. The four of us spent long summer evenings on their deck, laughing under the stars. We took vacations together, enjoying every minute. She was full of energy, very bright and a deeply dedicated apprentice of Jesus. Her death shattered me. She was only fifty-two, and left behind a husband and a seven-year-old son. I ached for days and suspect I will never get over it, but merely get through it.

A tragedy, to be sure.

But rumors of her demise are greatly exaggerated. She now rules and reigns in the heavens, and knowing Sheryl, she is probably running a small galaxy somewhere. I will see her again. And her dear husband, Doug, a dedicated Christ-follower, will also see her again and, in the meanwhile, survive, as well as young Paul, because God is good, and very near.

Death is the great enemy, but it has been defeated. Sin is the great destroyer, but it too has been defeated. Both of these menaces have been defeated by the greatest event the world has ever witnessed: the resurrection of Jesus.

Every single issue in life, every problem we face, every hope we have—absolutely everything hinges on the resurrection of Jesus.

That is a bold statement, but I have come to believe that it is true. Life's fundamental questions—such as, Who am I? What happens when we die? How do we grow in holiness in this life? What is the reason for our hope?—all find their answer in the resurrection.

Jesus' death and resurrection were God's divine victory over that which plagues us, giving us freedom and hope. But they are even more. The death and resurrection of Jesus are also our death and resurrection. Paul wrote,

> I have been crucified with Christ; and it is no longer I
> who live, but it is Christ who lives in me. And the life I

now live in the flesh I live by faith in the Son of God, who loved me and gave himself for me. (Galatians 2:19-20 NRSV)

The old me, the old Jim, has died. When I put my confidence in Jesus as the Son of God and resurrected Lord of all, my old way of living ended. Before I lived "with no God," and now I live a "with-God life." Before I was on my own, trying to establish my identity and worth. Now I am in intimate fellowship with "the Son of God, who loved me and gave himself for me." My worth has been established by Jesus, who died for me in order to have a relationship with me.

And it is all a gift from God. I did nothing to deserve it. He did not die merely to get me into heaven, but to get heaven into me. His life—pure and powerful—now lives in me. I am in Christ, and Christ is in me. Paul begins Colossians 3 with "Since, then, you have been raised with Christ," because that is the fundamental truth about who I am, and that truth determines how I live and where I will spend eternity. This truth affects my ethics. I do all I do (put away sin, put on holiness, give glory to God in all I do) because Jesus, and I, have been resurrected.

The rest of Colossians 3 shows us how Christians ought to live. Paul's admonitions (stop lying, bear each other's burdens, live in harmony, forgive and love each other, accept everyone) are all based on the co-resurrection his hearers have experienced. They are not a list of legalistic rules; they are expressions of how Christ-followers live because Jesus lives in them.

The glorious truth is that we can now begin putting sin to death! We can trust that our very lives are hidden with Jesus, safe and secure. We can build our lives on the hope of eternal bliss because Jesus paid and paved the way, and is seated at the right hand of God, praying for us.

What are you facing today? Trouble in your family? Financial hardship? The loss of something—a person, a relationship, a job, perhaps a dream? Believe it or not, the resurrection of Jesus is your answer. In Jesus' life, death and resurrection, God reconciled the world, overcame its evil with good, and stands as the ultimate reality about our world. Whatever we face, we do not face it alone, but with the One who now rules and reigns in the heavens, prays for us and will see to it that in the end we will laugh until it hurts, because the beauty of God is overwhelming.

Jesus is the King of the universe, the ruler of all. You and I and my dear friend Sheryl have been *raised* with him, alive to the world above, where he is. And since Jesus is now in the position of authority as the resurrected Lamb and Lion, nothing, absolutely nothing, can prevent our access to God and his glorious realm. That is why we live with no insecurity, either about our salvation or the final outcome of everything. God gets the last word. And God is good. And it is going to be well. All manner of things will be well.

At Sheryl's funeral one of her favorite songs was sung: "Give Me Jesus." The lyrics proclaim,

Oh when I come to die,
Oh when I come to die,
Oh when I come to die,
Give me Jesus.
Give me Jesus. Give me Jesus.
You can have all this world,
But give me Jesus.

That was her prayer, and that prayer was answered, in this life and in the next. She was given Jesus, because Jesus gave himself to her, and she was wise enough to accept the gift. The next time I see her we will laugh under the stars until our sides hurt.

Living into the Truth

As Christians we put a lot of focus on the cross. It is at the center of most churches and the subject of most sermons. We even wear it on necklaces. In contrast, little attention is paid to the resurrection. Without the resurrection, evil would have won. The resurrection is God's great YES to the world. Perhaps we would do well to have "empty tombs" on our necklaces. But short of that, we would do well to reflect on the victory of God that we see in the resurrection.

Take time to meditate on the empty tomb. Say to yourself, "He did it!" over and over. Dwell on the reality that death has been defeated, on the truth that you have been raised with Jesus and that you will never die. Read Matthew 27:61–28:20, which tells the story of how Jesus burst forth from the grave and began a revolution of love and power made perfect in surrender.

AFFIRMATION

Jesus rose from the grave. There is nothing I cannot rise from. Even death cannot hold me down. Nothing can separate me from the love of God in Christ Jesus.

PRAYER

Gracious Abba, thank you for sending your Son, Jesus, to die and to rise, to defeat sin and death and all that plagues humanity. His resurrection not only proves your victory but gives me new life, salvation and hope. Thank you.

REFLECTION

Have you known, and been living your Christian life from, this reality (that you died and rose with Jesus)? If not, why do you suppose it was never explained to you? What difference can this insight have in your life as an apprentice of Jesus?

What things from your life before being raised with Christ are you holding on to that are hindering you from experiencing the freedom given in Christ?

2

WITH

So if you have been raised **with** *Christ . . .*

COLOSSIANS 3:1 (NRSV)

For almost twenty years I had a beat-up, old, broken-down mower. Each spring I dreaded going to the shed and pulling it out and fighting it all summer. Two years ago it finally gave out, and it was time for a new mower. So I went eagerly to the hardware store and bought a brand new, self-propelled, state-of-the-art mower. It was a thing of beauty. It started with one pull. It mowed the grass with ease, and the self-propelled mechanism seemed to pull me along for the ride. I was no longer mowing; I was taking a stroll behind a powerful machine that practically mowed without me.

The following spring I went out to get the mower from the

shed, and there it was, all shiny and ready to eat grass. I began mowing, and about halfway through the backyard I noticed I was sweating profusely. My arms and legs were exhausted. I had two thoughts come into my mind: one, I am out of "mowing" shape, and two, this mower is really heavy and hard to maneuver. Then it hit me: I was not using the self-propelled mechanism. The mower, by itself, is rather heavy and hard to push and turn if you, like me, are not bright enough to squeeze the lever that activates the power drive. Once I squeezed the lever, behold, the mower took off without my effort, and I was once again along for a nice stroll.

My experience with the mower illustrates something true about the Christian life: when we have been raised with Christ, we are now "in Christ," and Christ is "in us"; we have a new capacity, a new energy, a new power to live the Christian life. It is activated not by squeezing a lever but by aligning our minds and hearts with the available power of the kingdom of God that is now among us and in us (Colossians 1:27). When we do, we find ourselves pulled along for a very nice ride. We work, but we don't sweat. We act, but a stronger, greater, quieter power is acting within and around us.

This whole idea can be summed up by one word: *with*. It is a small word, a boring preposition we almost always overlook. But it is a powerful word. I once heard a preacher talk about this little word, about how it's present—but overlooked—throughout the Bible. He talked about how God was *with* Abraham, how the Bible says God was *with* David and *with*

Esther and *with* Solomon and, most especially, *with* Jesus (Acts 10:38). In fact, one of Jesus' names is Immanuel, which means "God with us." We have a choice between two ways to live: with God or without God. The first way is like mowing with the self-propelled engine; the second is like mowing without it. The first way is easy; the second is hard.

I am not saying that life with God, or the with-God life, is without pain or struggle, but I am saying that the with-God life provides a strength we do not possess, so that no matter what we face—our joys or sorrows, our triumphs or temptations—we have a power at work within us that changes the way we live.

My greatest regret as a Christian is the fact that, for many, many years, I thought faith amounted to keeping a set of rules. My greatest source of frustration came from the fact that I tried, for many years, to live the Christian life by my own strength. Let me explain.

After I accepted Jesus as my Lord and Savior I found myself changing—from the inside. My inner world was shifting. New thoughts and new emotions came sprouting out like tulips in the spring. It was almost as if something was alive in me, perhaps what a pregnant woman feels like. I had these new cravings: I wanted to read the Bible, a book that previously had made no sense to me but now suddenly did make sense. And more than that, simply reading it made me feel strange things like peace and inspiration to do what it was telling me to do. I actually found myself wanting to go to church. Within a year or so I became part of organized Christianity.

I soon found myself faced with a lot of rules. I had older Christians tell me that Christians were forbidden from doing certain things (going to parties, having sex) and were commanded to do certain other things (read the Bible, pray). There was something in me that was drawn to this kind of rule keeping. It made sense. The problem was that I did not live up to the standards I professed to live by. Sure, I could pray and serve others, but I also found myself frustrated at trying to maintain the image when in reality I still got angry, still lusted and still wanted to go to parties, even if I didn't go. Mostly I was just faking it. I assumed God was frustrated with me, and I was miserable.

The solution came when I learned about my identity in Christ and the power of the kingdom of God. I had been thinking of myself as a sinner trying not to sin (try that paradox on for a while). I thought the kingdom of God was something I would experience in the next life. It turns out I was missing two essential ideas in Christianity: Christians are indwelt and empowered by Jesus, and we have access to a life with God (the kingdom of God) every moment of our lives. All those years I was trying to live the Christian life. And all those years I had it wrong. I cannot live the Christian life. I cannot make myself a Christian by keeping all of the rules.

Paul writes in Colossians 1:1, "So if you have been raised *with* Christ . . ." Notice the language: "you have been." It is a past act with present and continuous consequences. It is a reality, a truth, a completed act. This is who I really am, not because of what I do but because of what God has done. I really died with Jesus, and I really rose with him, and he really lives in me. Now I face each day with a choice: will I try to live the Christian life on my own (living from "the flesh," which is human power disconnected from God), or will I live in the power of God (living in "the Spirit").

When I walk in the Spirit I find strength I never knew I had access to, wisdom I never found in my own small brain and a joy I never imagined. I can do all of this because God is with me. And God is within you, calling you to live the Christian life not out of your own will power, which will always fail, but by the power of the Christ, through whom you can do all things, even more than you can ask or imagine.

LIVING INTO THE TRUTH

Today, or this week, engage in one of the most powerful exercises a Christian can do: practicing the presence of God. It's not difficult to do, but it is difficult to maintain. Simply call to mind that Jesus is with you this very moment, in whatever you are doing—in your meetings, in your work, in your planning, in your relationships. You are not alone. God is *with* you. You may want to try this for just twenty minutes or so at first as you develop this new and powerful habit.

One of the things I do to help me with this is to repeat the following short affirmation: "God is with me, here, now." I find that when I practice this I get a surge of inspiration that often leads to both calm and courage. The biggest struggle will be keeping your mind on the presence of God. You have trained your mind so long in the other way—the absence of God—that it will be hard to see and perceive in a new way. We have to learn "to live life on two levels," a phrase from the great Quaker author Thomas Kelly. On one level we simply go about our normal day (brushing our teeth, shopping, hanging out with friends), but on another level we can have an ongoing awareness of the presence of God. Don't force this, and don't feel bad when you stop thinking about God. But above all, don't give up. This is one of those exercises that can change your life in deep ways.

AFFIRMATION

God is with me in all that I do. I have strength, wisdom and all of the provision I need.

PRAYER

Gracious Abba, I do not know why you chose me, but you did. And I know that I do not have any strength on my own. But I also know I can do all things through you who gives me strength. Teach me how to walk with you every step of this day.

REFLECTION

What did you feel when you first discovered that God is with you?

In what areas of your life do you struggle to let God be with you? Why?

3

SEATED

*So if you have been raised with Christ, seek the things
that are above, where Christ is,* **seated** *at the right hand of God.*

COLOSSIANS 3:1 (NRSV)

For years I have recited the Apostles' Creed, the ancient declaration and formulation of the Christian faith, sometimes in church, sometimes in my private devotions. However, there is one phrase that, for a long time, I never understood:

> [Jesus] was crucified, died and was buried;
> he descended into hell;
> on the third day he rose again from the dead;
> he ascended into heaven,

and is *seated* at the right hand of God the Father
almighty;
from there he will come again to judge the living and
the dead.

What does it mean that Jesus is seated at the right hand of
God? Why is this important? I have probably heard a hundred
sermons on the life and death of Jesus, but not even one
sermon directly on this subject.

I would later learn that in the Bible, "to be seated" is a
metaphor for having finished one's work: *one is seated when
the work is completed.* So clearly Jesus must have completed
some work before he sat down. Hebrews 1:3 explains:

When he had made purification for sins, he *sat* down at
the right hand of the Majesty on high. (NRSV)

What Jesus had finished was the work of reconciling the
world to God. What he had accomplished was the forgiveness
of sins for all people, for all time, past, present and future.
Jesus' work on the cross was so perfect, so complete, that he
will not have to do it over again. Jesus also rose from the dead,
defeating death and imparting his life to us: we have been
raised with Christ.

The work Jesus did—from the incarnation, to living a
perfect life we could not live, to freely offering himself on
the cross, to the resurrection—was the perfect completion of
the triune effort to bring the world into a life of intimacy

with the Father, the Son and the Holy Spirit. In other words—
he finished the job! He can now sit down. He does not need
to do it again. As he himself said on the cross, "It is finished."
This is very good news for us. But there is also another
reason he is seated.

A Priest Who Prays

Jesus completely finished the work of reconciliation, but that
does not mean he is up in heaven taking a long nap. One of
the most beautiful parts of the theology of the ascension is
that Jesus is now praying for us. Jesus is our great High Priest
who intercedes for us. Having been reconciled with us
through his death, Jesus is now laboring for our healing
through his prayer: "Who is to condemn? It is Christ Jesus,
who died, yes, who was raised, who is at the right hand of
God, who indeed intercedes for us" (Romans 8:34 NRSV).

What does this mean for you and for me? It means that not
only do we stand forever forgiven, but Jesus is also forever
praying for us. And what is he praying for? He is praying that
you and I would be completely new people, people in whom
he can make his home.

When Paul asks the Colossians to "seek the things that
are above, where Christ is, seated at the right hand of God,"
he is urging them to reflect on the wonder of Jesus, the
Lamb of God who took away the sins of the world (John
1:29), and the splendor of Jesus, the High Priest who now
prays for us. This is how God is "making all things new."

The glorious Trinity (Father, Son and Spirit) is on a mission to transform every one of us. That does not happen by anything we do of ourselves. Jesus did it all. And Jesus does it all—by continuing to pray for each of us. But we do participate in this transformation. We set our minds on these truths: we are forgiven, and Jesus is praying for us. And when Jesus prays, things happen. He will not stop until he has made us all new people.

LIVING INTO THE TRUTH

Today, or this week, spend time reflecting on the two truths explained in this chapter: Jesus paid it all, and Jesus is now praying for you. You may find, as I did, that this will influence the way you pray. Reflecting on the first truth changed my time of confession from me trying to remember all of my sins and list them before God in the hopes of having them erased. They are erased. Confession now involves discussing my sins with God. I reflect on my recent actions, asking God to help me see where I have sinned. Often a thought, word or deed comes to mind, and God and I then dialogue about it. We talk about why I felt drawn to sin in that way and about how I can, in light of his grace, truth and power, behave differently next time. This shift has been very freeing, and healing, in my life with God.

Setting my mind on the second truth (Jesus praying for me) has also changed the way I pray. I now pray *with* Jesus, not simply *to* Jesus. Jesus is interceding for me (and you) so

I offer my prayers for my family, friends and myself with Jesus, to our heavenly Father. This changes the content and the dynamic of prayer. Knowing Jesus is praying with me allows me to ask him what we should be praying for. Like his first disciples, we say to Jesus, "Teach us to pray." And simply knowing I am praying with Jesus gives me great courage. Together, we are making all things new.

AFFIRMATION

Jesus paid it all, and now he is praying for all. This is another reason that nothing can separate me from the love of God in Christ Jesus.

PRAYER

Precious Jesus, thank you for taking away all of my sins, even mine, for now and for all time. Your work in that regard is done, and I now live in the peace of the finality of the cross. Thank you. And thank you for praying for me. Help me to know that when I pray, I am not praying alone. Amen.

REFLECTION

What difference does it make knowing that Jesus is praying for you? How does that make you feel?

4

SET

Set your minds on things that are above,
not on things that are on earth.

<small>COLOSSIANS 3:2 (NRSV)</small>

My car stereo, like most people's, has two different bands in which to receive radio signals: AM and FM. I have no idea how it works or why it works; I just know that when I push the AM button my radio picks up AM stations, and when I push the FM button it changes to radio stations on the FM frequency. One day I noticed that the preset AM station was a Christian radio program where a preacher was reading the Bible. When I switched over to FM it was a pop music station that was playing a song with raunchy lyrics all about money, sex and materialism. I switched back to the AM station, where Romans 8 was being read:

> For those who live according to the flesh set their *minds* on the things of the flesh, but those who live according to the Spirit set their *minds* on the things of the Spirit. (Romans 8:5 NRSV)

Then it occurred to me: these two stations were a perfect example of that verse. One station was proclaiming the things of "the flesh," and the other station was set on "the Spirit."

Which station would I listen to? If I listened to the FM station, I would be exposing my mind to the values of the kingdom of this world as it proclaimed the joys of engaging in illicit sex, drinking expensive champagne and getting rich. If I listened to the AM station, I would be listening to a preacher talk about the values of the kingdom of God: surrender, trust and faith.

When it comes down to it, living the Christian life is simply a matter of where we *set* our minds. Every waking moment we have a choice about where, and on what, we will set our minds. That is something we are free to do. Having been raised with Christ and forgiven forever, and having Jesus with us in all that we do, the primary practice of living as a Christian boils down to what we think about, what we dwell on, what values we keep before our minds, what truths (or lies) we have in our consciousness.

I am not saying that in order to be a good Christian we

have to listen to Christian radio all day, or that we should never listen to secular music. Black and white rules always fail in these matters. I am also not saying we should read the Bible all day or that we should never read non-Christian books or magazines.

I am saying that where we set our minds and what we think about has a large impact on how we live, how we feel and how we react to the world around us. *We have a choice, and that choice will affect us.* If I steep my mind in "things above," I find myself energized and encouraged. If I focus my consciousness on "things that are on earth," I find myself frustrated and disappointed.

What are these things "above," or "of the Spirit," that we are called to set our minds on? I think it means things like the unending and unchanging love of God; the provision and power of God; the forgiveness of sins; the fact that God is with us in all we face; the adoption into the family of God for all believers; the intimate compassion of God that moves us to cry out, "Abba," an Aramaic term of endearment for an earthly father, probably best translated as "dear father." Simply reflecting on the fact that I have died and risen with Christ changes my countenance. Setting my mind on the mind-blowing reality that Jesus is praying for me creates a sense of awe. And it makes me glad.

The things of the Spirit are characterized by qualities such as truth, goodness and beauty. Paul put it this way:

Finally, beloved, whatever is true, whatever is honorable, whatever is just, whatever is pure, whatever is pleasing, whatever is commendable, if there is any excellence and if there is anything worthy of praise, *think* about these things. (Philippians 4:8 NRSV)

Justice. Purity. Excellence. These are the "things of the Spirit" and what we are called to think about. When we do, we find our souls being nourished.

AM OR FM?

Each day I have to choose where I will "tune" my mind. Will it be on the presence of a loving, smiling Abba who is with me, or will it be on a harsh and cold world where money, sex and power are viewed as the ways to happiness? The best hours and days of my life are the ones where I keep the dial set on the kingdom of heaven. It is a small act in some ways, but the impact on my life is enormous.

Making a choice to reflect on the truths of God that I know (God is good; God is beautiful; God is true; God is self-sacrificing, etc.) and contemplating them as much as possible throughout my day helps me see the world I live in with a new perspective. I see my culture through the lens of the kingdom of God. Doing this also helps me change channels and alter conversations when it becomes clear that no real good is going to come from what I am about to allow past my ear-gates and eye-gates and through my mind-gate. I have a choice about what to steep my mind in, which will shape my soul, for good or for ill. I vastly prefer the good.

LIVING INTO THE TRUTH

Today set aside ten minutes to simply reflect on some of the "things of the Spirit." They are (to name a few):

- the unending and unchanging love of God
- the provision and power of God
- the forgiveness of sins
- the fact that God is with us in all we face
- the adoption into the family of God for all believers

Pick one or two of these and simply take a few minutes to tune your mind to these truths. Think about God's steadfast love. Meditate on how much God cares for you and your needs. Reflect on the mercy of God's forgiveness. Contemplate the mystery and majesty of God being with you—and simply practice his presence. Finally, steep your mind in the wonder of being adopted into the family of God.

AFFIRMATION

Each day I must decide where to set my mind. If I set it on the truths of God I will be happy and holy and strong. Therefore, I will choose to set my mind on the things of the Spirit this day.

PRAYER

I am not strong, Lord. I need your help in this matter of where I set my mind. Help me, Holy Spirit, to keep my thoughts on things above.

REFLECTION

How have you experienced the difference between setting your mind on the flesh versus setting your mind on the things of the Spirit?

If you could only set your mind on one truth of God (mentioned above), what would it be? Why?

5

HIDDEN

For you died, and your life is now
hidden *with Christ in God.*

COLOSSIANS 3:3

I had a student in several of my classes named Olga who was born and raised in Russia. Just before graduation she came to my office to give me a gift. It was a type of doll popular in Russia, called a matryoshka doll, or babushka doll. It is a nesting doll, made of wood, in which a set of dolls of decreasing size are placed one inside the other. Olga's doll had just two dolls. Hidden inside the smaller doll was a piece of delicious chocolate. I thanked her for this kind gift, and kept it on my desk as a reminder of Olga and the growth of her faith while she was in college. Not raised as a practicing

Christian, she found Christianity intriguing and took several classes from me even though they were outside of her major. Every time I noticed the doll I smiled and thanked God for the privilege of being a teacher.

A few years later I found myself looking at the doll, and I had a small epiphany. I had been memorizing Colossians 3, and the first four verses all talk about dying and rising with Christ and how our lives are "hidden" in Christ. This concept was hard to understand. How did I die with Jesus? How did I rise with him? How was my life "in" Christ? And does it really matter? Apparently it does, because Paul wrote so much about it. I discovered that Paul uses the phrases "in Christ" and "Christ in us" eighty-nine times. *That is a lot,* I thought, *so it must be important, even if I do not understand what it really means.*

I realized that the Russian dolls illustrate both kinds of "in." When I focus on the bigger doll hiding the smaller doll, I think about how I am "in Christ." Jesus is like the bigger doll, and I live and move within him. This is very comforting and encouraging as I think about how I, by God's grace, have received all that Jesus is and does and has done—forgiveness, reconciliation, life, healing, power, wisdom. When I focus on the smaller doll inside the bigger doll, sometimes I reflect on how Christ is "in me." Again, by God's grace, I have new life in me; the very life and power that raised Jesus from the dead lives in me. I don't know how this works, but I know that it is a reality by the ways Jesus works in and through me.

But what did it mean that I had died and risen with Jesus, that my life was now "hidden with Christ in God" (Colossians 3:3)? Did this mean anything to my daily life as a Christ-follower?

We are all desperate to find the answers to two important questions: Who am I? and Where am I? The deeper questions behind those questions are, Am I significant? and Am I safe? In my weaker moments, I sometimes wonder if I am valuable, and try to find ways to make myself feel significant. And I get scared now and then—the economy, the wars, the uncertainty of the job market and a host of other crises big and small make me cower at times. Will everything be okay? My prayers are often simply, "Help me make it through this day, God."

Then the small epiphany came. The phrase "hidden with Christ in God" had been bouncing around my brain, and suddenly I saw a physical illustration of that spiritual reality in that Russian doll. Just as the smaller doll was hidden in the larger doll, so my very life is hidden in Jesus. I am like the smaller doll. I cannot see this life, but I know it is real. I know it each time I experience God with me. But here is what became evident to me: if Christ is in me, and I am in him, I am significant, and I am safe. I found the answer to those two desperate questions, and I did not find it by doing something great or looking great or showing off my skills. I did not find it by having a good insurance policy or retirement plan or a car with five airbags; nor is it found by getting great grades at school or promotions at work, fitting in socially or finding the perfect mate. I find significance and safety in the fact that my life is hidden with Christ in God.

My identity is something I work hard to establish: teacher, writer, speaker and so on. I assume that people think I am important because of this identity. When people hear that I have published books, I can see on their faces that they are impressed, and to be honest, I feel good when this happens. I smile inwardly but try not to show it lest they think I am prideful (which I am, but I don't want them to see it). But those things are ephemeral, constantly changing and thus precarious. What would happen if I lost my job? Or if no one wanted to publish my writing or hear me speak? Who would I be?

From Colossians 3, and the Russian doll, I got a clear picture: I am one in whom Christ dwells. And if he willingly gave his life for me out of love and has taken my life into his, then he must also be crazy about me. God, I then thought, does not merely love me, he actually likes me. So my identity became even more wonderful: I am Jim in whom Christ dwells and delights. This is a powerful thought. As I said it over and over to myself I felt a kind of energy pulsing through me. This identity is not precarious—it will never change. I did not earn it, and I cannot lose it. It is based on what God has done for me, not on what I have done for God. I fret about how committed (or not committed) I am to Jesus. What really matters is that Jesus is fully committed to me. My life is hidden inside of his.

Because my life is hidden in his, I am strong: "I can do all things through [Christ] who strengthens me" (Philippians 4:13 NRSV). Jesus said I could do greater things than he did (John 14:12), which is far more than I would attempt without his encouragement. What are you facing this day? You are not alone. Is it a problem at work? Are you wrestling with finding your identity apart from your accomplishments? Are you worried about your children? Do you feel anxious about the future? Remember who you are: you are one in whom Christ dwells and delights. Remember where you are: you are "in Christ," safe and secure. And remember what you are capable of: you can do all things through Christ.

You are significant.

You are strong.

More significant and stronger than you know.

LIVING INTO THE TRUTH

The central truth in this chapter is about your *place* as a Christian and is summarized in this very powerful statement: "My life is hidden with Christ in God." This is true, even if you do not fully believe it. Commit this simple phrase to memory, and as you go about your day, try to say it several times. I like to say it as I walk or drive, gently speaking this truth to my mind and my heart. My body seems to be energized by this practice; I find myself feeling strong and positive. Remember, this is not wishful thinking—you are not making this true by saying it. This is "reality therapy," placing your mind firmly in truth. As you do it, you will begin to see yourself, and God, in a different way.

AFFIRMATION

My life is safe, secure and hidden in Christ Jesus. I have nothing to fear this day, or any day.

PRAYER

Thank you, Jesus, for establishing my life in you. May I walk in the glorious freedom that nothing can harm me. Help me to live each breath today in wonder over this great truth.

REFLECTION

Have you ever felt really alone? If so, how might the truth of this verse bring comfort to you?

In what "earthly" ways do you try to find safety, security and significance?

6

LIFE

When Christ, who is your **life** *. . .*

COLOSSIANS 3:4

The other day I was driving behind a pick-up truck with a bumper sticker that read, "Fishing is my life!" I thought to myself, *This guy must be crazy about fishing. I wonder how often he fishes.* Then the actual phrasing hit me: fishing *is* my life. I then thought, *Does he really believe that?* It does not say, "Fishing is what I love most!" or even "Fishing is the most important part of my life." The driver is saying that his very life is fishing, that the source of his existence is fishing itself. This is not merely a hyperbole; it is a statement of being.

And it is clearly false. With all due respect to his passion for fishing, fishing is an activity one engages in, not the very source of life. Fishing did not bring him into existence, nor does it continue to make his heart beat and his lungs take in air. Perhaps what he wanted to communicate was, "My whole reason to live is to fish." If that is his philosophy, his feeling, then I cannot doubt he is telling the truth. But if he were my friend and he asked me what I thought about his philosophy, I would tell him it is misguided, that he has mistaken a hobby for his maker.

JESUS THE CREATOR OF ALL BIOLOGICAL LIFE

In Colossians 3:4, Paul uses the same phrasing as the bumper sticker: Christ *is* your life. Jesus is the true and genuine source of life, not just for Christians. Jesus is the divine Word of God, the Logos, who created and sustains the universe: "In the beginning was the Word, and the Word was with God, and the Word was God. He was with God in the beginning. Through him all things were made; without him nothing was made that has been made" (John 1:1-3). All things, it says, were made by Jesus. The sun and the stars, the earth and the rings of Jupiter, the Rocky Mountains and the deserts of Africa, the birds and the fishes, every rose bush, river and person were made by Jesus. And that includes the fellow with the bumper sticker.

Earlier in Colossians, Paul wrote of Jesus, "For in him all things were created: things in heaven and on earth, visible and invisible, whether thrones or powers or rulers or authorities; all things have been created through him and for him. He is before all things, and in him all things hold together"

(Colossians 1:16-17). From this it is clear: Jesus is not only the source of everything, but all things are also held together by him. This means that the atoms and molecules that make up your physical body are upheld by Jesus. Right now, Jesus is literally sustaining you, holding you together. Our biological life was created, and is sustained, by Jesus. The bowl of cereal you ate that is now being broken down by your body in order to incorporate its caloric energy? That was Jesus' arrangement. Sadly, few Christians know what John and Paul knew and thus do not give him thanks.

JESUS THE GIVER OF ETERNAL LIFE

In addition to our bodily life, Jesus is also the giver of our spiritual life. The Greek word *bios* refers to our biological life, but John used the word *zoe* to describe spiritual life. Our very spirits were designed to be infused by *zoe*. When we come into this world we are physically alive but spiritually dead. We have *bios*, but we do not have *zoe*. We receive *zoe* when we receive Jesus by faith: "But these are written that you may believe that Jesus is the Messiah, the Son of God, and that by believing you may *have life* in his name" (John 20:31). If, however, we do not put our trust in Jesus we do not have this *zoe*: "Whoever has the Son has life; whoever does not have the Son of God does not *have life*" (1 John 5:12).

When I put my confidence in Jesus and began living as his apprentice, a new life emerged in my being. My spirit, like Lazarus' body, went from death to life. And that *zoe* life is eternal, safe and secure, hidden with Jesus. I live by this eternal life now, and I will enter fully into it when I take my last breath on earth. Jesus is not only the artisan who crafted our physical life, not only the one who sustains and holds all things together, he is also the sacrificial lamb who died and rose that we might have eternal spiritual life. We would never have come into existence if it were not for Jesus, and we would have no hope of eternal life if not for his grace. That is why Paul says in Colossians 3:4, "Christ . . . is your life."

James S. Stewart writes, "The New Testament never speaks of eternal life as something that begins only at death, something new into which death suddenly ushers us: that is quite unscriptural. On the contrary, the New Testament always speaks of eternal life as something that begins here and now, on this side of the grave, something that exists as a present possession of those who are in fellowship with God." True life, eternal life, the life we were designed to possess, is a gift from Jesus for this life, not merely the next. That fact alone is missed by so many Christians, and as a consequence many miss out on the richness of life here on earth.

JESUS IS MY LIFE

Only Jesus can be our life. A line in Colossians 1:16, which I quoted earlier, says, "all things have been created through him and *for* him." Your life and mine were not only created *by* Jesus, they were created *for* Jesus. The rocks and the trees, the ducks and the Milky Way were all created for Jesus. The heavens and the earth and all of its inhabitants constantly give glory to God—except one species: human beings. We have the freedom to choose to give God glory or not. We can reject God. We can deny God's existence. But most of us, especially those reading this book, desire to give him glory and honor. If so, how do we do that?

We begin with gratitude. We turn to God and say, "Thank you, blessed and beautiful Trinity—Father, Son and Spirit. Thank you for making me. Thank you for sustaining me. Thank you for giving your life for me, so that I can have eternal life in you." Then we begin to see all of our life as being centered in Jesus, with Jesus as our top priority.

Is there something more important in our lives than Jesus? If so, perhaps we will need to make an adjustment. When Christ becomes not only our life but the thing we live for, we discover the reality of what he came to bring: not merely life, but abundant life (John 10:10). Jesus truly *is* our life.

LIVING INTO THE TRUTH

This week, engage in whatever soul-training exercises nourish your spirit, but do so with an attitude of gratitude—for these practices that connect you to God but also that God, in his grace, is sustaining you. Just as you say "grace" before a meal, giving thanks for the physical sustenance you are about to receive, pause to say "grace" before you pray or read the Bible or go to worship, giving thanks for the spiritual sustenance you are about to receive.

AFFIRMATION

Just as my body needs to take in energy from outside of itself in order to live, so also my spirit needs to take in the energy of God himself in order to thrive. Today I will seek that energy by opening myself up to God and his kingdom.

PRAYER

Gracious Abba, thank you for creating me, but even more so, this day I thank you for sustaining me, in body, soul and spirit. Give me a heart of gratitude for all of the grace you give me each day.

REFLECTION

If someone simply watched you living your life, what might they conclude *is* your life? What would they say is the thing you live for?

What are the most spiritually nourishing practices for you? Why are they so helpful to you?

7

REVEALED

When Christ who is your life is revealed,
then you also will be **revealed** *with him in glory.*

COLOSSIANS 3:4 (NRSV)

I am an avid sports fan. I often record the games of my favorite teams so I can watch them later. (Skipping commercials is wonderful in itself!) In order to avoid learning the outcome before I watch the game I have to steer clear of television sets that might show the score. I also have to tell people who might know the outcome not to tell me, or even hint to me, how the game ends. No matter how hard I try, though, now and then I accidentally learn about the outcome of a game before I get to watch it. One time, my favorite baseball team was playing in a big playoff game, and I learned the final score before I actually watched it (my team won!). I still watched the game and at times found myself actually nervous (old habits die hard), but kept reminding myself, *Remember, we win. You know how this ends, Jim, so don't get discouraged.*

Paul wrote to the Colossians, "When Christ . . . is revealed, then you also will be revealed with him in glory." Paul is pointing to the return of Christ, something that United Methodists, along with several other traditions, affirm in the communion liturgy: "Christ has died, Christ is risen, *Christ will come again*" (italics mine). The return of Jesus has been an important belief for his people from the beginning to the present. We live in a broken, troubled world. Things around us fall apart; marriages and governments and economies collapse. We find ourselves making a mess of our lives from time to time and it forces us to wonder, *Are we going to make it? Will everything be alright?*

What Paul is saying in Colossians 3:4 is the same truth I told myself while watching my tape-delayed baseball game: "Remember—we win." The return of Jesus will be the full and final consummation of a battle that has already been won (on the cross and in the tomb). In this verse, Paul is counseling the Colossians to set their minds on this truth. He wants them to think about that glorious day and to know—to know with certainty and not merely wish for—how it all ends. There is a word for this certainty in a good future: hope.

Hope is not wishful thinking; it is being certain that the future is bright.

Hope gives us confidence. Hope gives us assurance. Hope enables us to trust, to have faith in the present moment, no matter how bleak. Hope gives us peace in the midst of strife. Hope bring us joy in times of sadness. Confidence, assurance, trust, faith, peace and joy are things that make life wonderful, that give us strength and courage, realities that make us sleep well and work hard. As long as we have hope we will never give up.

Only the gospel, the good news, of Jesus can make this happen. The rest of the world looks to advances in technology and medicine and politics and hopes that new gadgets and pills and bills will ensure a happy life. But they always let us down. They cannot make a dent on the reality that, while defeated, the devil, sin and death still exert a partial force over human life. Only the reality of the resurrection, and its final consummation in Christ's return, can bring us the confidence, assurance, trust, faith, hope, peace and joy that will make our lives magnificent, the kind of life we were made to live.

This fact about the future makes an enormous difference in the present, because in the present we experience setbacks, losses, dark valleys and disappointments, and they can overwhelm us. Focusing on the future glory that awaits us affects how we cope with the present struggles we face. Things may look bleak now, but one day we will stand with Jesus, who has been glorified, and we will be glorified with him. The radiance of Jesus—who is our life—will be flowing out of us.

Everything we have suffered through in this life will melt away in this moment of glory.

A few years ago several friends and I threw a surprise birthday party for a dear friend who had experienced a number of difficulties over the past several years. She had lost dear family members and gone through a painful divorce. Each time I saw her she had a pained look on her face, but she did her best to be positive and not complain. We planned the party for months, and when the big night came we all crammed ourselves into a room at a local restaurant where she thought she would be dining with a friend. We had a huge birthday cake aflame with candles. When she came through that door and we all yelled, "Surprise!" and then sang happy birthday, tears flowed down her cheeks. It was a beautiful sight. The pain of recent years faded in this moment of glory. She knew she was loved, and she glowed.

That is the image we need to see when reading Colossians 3:4. On the day when Jesus takes us in his arms, our life will be celebrated. It may be at our moment of death, or it may be in this life, should he return before our earthly life ends. But that day will come. We can be certain. Not because of what we have done or deserved, but because Christ, who is our very life, gets the last word.

Until then, we must remind ourselves each day that we win. It makes all the difference. There is nothing we will face today—illness, loss, divorce, death—that will not be overcome in the final victory of Jesus. And this is not wishful thinking.

Jesus' resurrection secured this reality. If he rose from the dead, can he not also subdue all creation in final victory? The whole of the cosmos—the cosmos he himself made—will fall back into his hands and under his reign. It is a certainty. He won, and because we are in him, we win. For sure.

LIVING INTO THE TRUTH

The small victories of our lives are one area we see evidence of the final victory of Jesus—the times when we choose to love instead of hate, to forgive instead of hold a grudge, to be kind when being mean would be the usual course of action. In those moments we catch a glimpse of the victory he has already won. So this day, choose to perform an intentional act of kindness as evidence that you are on the winning side.

Acts of kindness also have a way of changing our perspective and reminding us that even though there is a lot of anger and selfishness in the world (and in us), something bigger and better is going on: love. When we do an act of kindness, we are demonstrating the truth that God is good and that, ultimately, God wins—which means we win as well. Do a simple act of kindness today and show the world whose side you are on.

AFFIRMATION

No matter what life brings me today, I know how it ends, and who wins. Therefore I walk in complete confidence, without any fear.

PRAYER

Gracious Abba, thank you for securing our final victory and for the certainty that we will be revealed with you in glory. Our world is full of much pain and suffering, and it makes our souls weary. But knowing that you get the last word and that all will be well gives us energy and courage. Thank you. Amen.

REFLECTION

Think of a time, or several times, in your life when a situation looked bleak, but in the end things worked out. Describe what happened and how it affected you.

How can knowing that in the end we will be with Jesus in glory affect how you live the days of your life until then?

You

*Put to death, therefore, whatever in **you** is earthly.*

Several years ago a friend of mine, who is a guitar aficionado, gave me a very valuable guitar. It is an Eric Clapton–signed, limited-edition guitar. When he gave it to me my friend spent twenty minutes describing in great detail each part of the guitar, explaining why it was so special. The wood is from Brazil and is very rare. The handmade construction of the guitar is superior to most, he pointed out, showing me subtle things I never would have noticed. When I got home I did a little research on the guitar to see what its original price had been. I was stunned to find out that the guitar I had just brought into my home was worth more than my car.

For weeks I was afraid to touch it. I would take it out and stare at it. Eventually I started to play it, and it sounded beautiful, unlike any guitar I had ever played. I am actually a pretty poor guitar player, but this guitar had such a nice sound that even I sounded like I could play. After each time I played it, I would carefully look it over, make sure I had not marred it and, more often than not, would take out my special guitar polish and cloth, give it a nice cleaning and return it to its plush, green-velvet-lined case. As instructed, I keep it in an even-temperature room.

I have two other guitars, old and beat up and not worth more than a hundred dollars combined. They do not have cases but lean against the wall in my daughter's playroom. If they get banged around, I don't care much. One day my daughter, Hope, had a friend over to play, and I overheard them in the kitchen talking about playing the guitar. Her friend was just learning to play. They went downstairs and I forgot about them for a moment as I read the newspaper. Then a light went on: guitars . . . eleven-year-old girls . . . they could be banging on my special guitar! I quickly ran downstairs and was relieved to see them playing my two old, beat-up guitars. "Whew," I said, and Hope replied, "Dad, I never touch your special guitar—you made me promise never to open the case unless you are with me."

In that moment I realized just how special that guitar is to me. I take great care of it, and I would never willingly subject it to harm. It is sacred to me, a fine work of art, so naturally I treat it with respect. Oddly enough, that is precisely Paul's reasoning about sin in the life of a Christ-follower. It is hard to notice at first, but if you look closely at his counsel in Colossians 3, you can see it. It is found in a single, often overlooked word: *therefore.*

For the first four verses (Colossians 3:1-4) Paul has been talking about *who we are.* He has been describing our identity. And he then reinforces its importance by telling us to set our hearts and minds on these truths. He says, "You died and rose with Jesus. He now lives in you, and your life is safe and secure in him. Get that in your head, and keep it there all the time. Remember who you are." Then comes the *therefore*: "Put to death, *therefore,* whatever in you is earthly" (Colossians 3:5).

Over the next several verses Paul tells us what those "earthly" things are: sexual immorality, lust, evil desires, greed, anger, rage, malice, slander, abusive language and lying. Every Christian knows we are not supposed to do these kinds of things, but very few know the real reason why. Most people think we should stop doing these things because God will be mad at us. So they try, using their willpower, to get rid of these kinds of behaviors, which leads to failure and frustration. It is certainly not Paul's approach. He never says, "Hey, stop doing these things or God will be angry and will punish you." Instead he says simply, "Remember who you are, and act accordingly."

So, who are we? We are in Jesus, and Jesus is in us. We have been infused with an eternal life that is hidden with

Christ, in God, safe and secure. We are sacred and holy, of immense worth, finely crafted, purified by the blood of the Lamb. We were bought with a great price. *Therefore,* our behavior should reflect our identity.

I find it so discouraging when I hear Christians describe themselves as "sinners." I will say to them, "If you are a sinner, then sin would be normative behavior for you, right?" They shrug and say, "Yes, that describes me. Thank the Lord for his grace and mercy." I then ask, "If sin is normative behavior for you, then why does sin hurt you so much? And if sin is normative, then why does the Bible tell us to stop?"

Paul addresses his letters "to the saints," not "the sinners." He knew that they were not sinless, but he also knew the deep truth that Christ Jesus had transformed their very being, and that by virtue of being people "in whom Christ dwells and delights" they were saints, sacred and special.

The key to Christlike living and Christlike loving is knowing your sacred value and worth. Just as I would never consider throwing my special guitar in the mud or scratching it up, so we should also never allow our sacred souls and bodies to wallow in sin. Anger and immorality, greed and deception, drunkenness and fornication are ways we desecrate the temples that we are.

The nineteenth-century Orthodox priest John of Kronstadt would go out into the streets each morning and lift up the drunken men who had slept in the gutters, saying to them, "This is beneath your dignity. You were meant to house the fullness of God." He did not say, "You rotten sinner, shape up!" Instead, he reminded them who they were. They were designed to inhabit God.

Sin is beneath us, unworthy of us, and can only mar and scar our souls. That is the right way to look at sin. It is not something we were made for. That is precisely why Paul instructs us to put it to death.

As I mentioned, I am not a good guitar player. Not long ago a friend of mine, who is an excellent guitar player, came over to see my beautiful guitar. He asked if he could play it, and I said sure. When he began to play it, the richness, the tone and the beauty of its sound filled the room. I later thought of how that, too, is like our situation. We are not only not made for sin, we are made to be "played" by our Lord, a virtuoso musician. When I say to Jesus, "Take my life and let it be consecrated, Lord, to thee," he takes my life and produces beautiful sound.

LIVING INTO THE TRUTH

Today, or sometime this week, reflect on your nature as a sacred vessel, created by God and designed to be consecrated to God. One of the practices I find helpful is to look at my hands and my feet. I stare at them for a few minutes, looking at how marvelously designed they are. And I think about what they were designed for. They were not designed for sin, but to be consecrated to God and placed under his care and control.

I also enjoy singing (to myself!) that beautiful hymn by Francis Havergal, "Take My Life and Let It Be." I sing it slowly and reflect on the lyrics: take my moments . . . take my lips . . . take my voice . . . take my feet. Set your mind on these truths. I suspect you will see sin in a whole new light, not as something you ought to try to stop but as something you would never want to do in light of who you are.

AFFIRMATION

I am sacred and special, a holy vessel, a temple of Jesus. Sin has no power over me, and it can only harm me. *Therefore*, I have no interest in it.

PRAYER

Gracious Abba, I need your help to see myself as you see me. I forget who I am and find myself drawn to sin. But in your eyes it is beneath my dignity. Help me to see it rightly, and therefore naturally turn from it.

REFLECTION

How do you feel when you think of yourself as God's precious, valuable instrument designed to be played by him?

In Christian settings what messages have you received about your sacred worth?

MORTIFY

Mortify *therefore your members [bodies]*
which are upon the earth.

*E*ach year my favorite sports magazine sends out its annual swimsuit issue. This issue has nothing to do with sports and, frankly, nothing to do with swimsuits. It is nothing more than scantily clad models lying on exotic beaches, bearing as much skin as possible. It is not created to advance the field of fashion or even to sell swimsuits. It has one sole purpose: to allow men to lust without too much guilt. It is, after all, a sports magazine. And the women are not *completely* naked. Each year the magazine is bombarded with mail from readers who either praise or rail against this annual issue.

I have subscribed to this magazine since I was thirteen. I remember my parents discussing what to do with the swimsuit issue when it arrived and overhearing my mom say something about it being "inappropriate for a young boy." I never saw the issue when it came that week, but a few months later I went to my dad's room to fetch the shoe-shine kit in his valet, and there it was, hidden from plain sight. I later sneaked into his room when my parents were not around and ogled the bikini-clad beauties. I felt a twinge in my conscience, and the fact that my father had hidden it added to my sense that I was doing something forbidden. But it was, after all, a sports magazine. I would do this every year for the next five years. Then something happened. I began following Christ.

For many, many years, that annual swimsuit issue became a source of anxiety for me: would I get rid of it (which I should), or would I skim it with a case of mild shame? After years of struggle and failure, I made a simple and clear decision: the moment I see it in our mailbox, without hesitation, I will walk straight to the trash bin and deposit it, never looking back. I have done precisely this for the last several years.

I have learned that temptation is easier to deal with at its onset, before it has a chance to grow into something more powerful. For many years I worried about receiving the swimsuit issue, and even prayed ahead of time that I would deal with it in a godly way. My "old self" was still alive and well and, frankly, looking forward to it.

It was St. Augustine who famously prayed, "Lord, make me chaste . . . but not yet." The reason for the "not yet" part of the prayer, I have come to realize, is that for many of us life seems dull compared with the enticement of sin, which then makes sin seem all the more exciting. We know sin is wrong, but we cannot imagine having joy without it. I actually wanted to sin, but knew that it was wrong, which caused internal turmoil.

As I increasingly became caught up in the joy and wonder of living in the highly fulfilling kingdom of God, and more keenly aware of my sacred worth, sin became less interesting. My decision to walk to the trash bin was preceded by many years of setting my mind and heart on the goodness and beauty of God, which made sin, in turn, seem ugly. I was discovering the deep joy available to me as I joined with Christ in kingdom life. The sin that had seemed so interesting had little to offer in comparison.

The best way to deal with sin is to give it no place in our lives. There is a very strong word used in the King James translation of Colossians 3:5: "*Mortify* therefore your members which are upon the earth." To "mortify" means "put it to death" or, more directly, "kill it."

Sin is like a mortgage, which is literally the slow death of your house debt (*mort* = death). Little by little, we are putting our debt to death. It is much the same way with sin. You cannot exterminate it. I can at any time turn away from God and put myself on the throne of my life, which always manifests itself in sin. God is not going to take away my capacity to turn from him.

The way we mortify sin is to refuse to let it enter our minds and hearts by keeping our hearts and minds on the things above. This does not mean that we have to live every waking moment in a religious trance, but rather that we make a clear decision that sin is not something we want in our lives, and that when we see it coming, we will not let it in the door.

A woman who is a teacher said to me recently, "I just struggle so much with gossip." I said, "When does this happen?" She said, "Every day in the teacher's lounge." I said, "Pray before you enter the lounge, and when you first hear gossip, as far as you are able, redirect the conversation to something positive. If you cannot, then slip away." A few weeks later she said, "You know what, that really worked. Thanks! I never knew it was so simple."

What she did was to mortify the sin of gossip. For years, she said, she tried and failed; but that was precisely because she tried to battle it with her *will*, and sin always defeats will power alone. By planning for it and refusing to enter into sin's arena, she killed it. That is why the key is to kill temptation early. Temptation becomes sin only if we let it in, and sin can only "exercise dominion" if we let it grow up. James describes this process in his epistle:

> Each person is tempted when they are dragged away by their own evil desire and enticed. Then, after desire has

conceived, it gives birth to sin; and sin, when it is full-grown, gives birth to death. (James 1:14-15)

Temptation is like a baby snake, barely harmful and easy to kill. A full-grown snake is very dangerous and hard to get rid of. In the same way, when a temptation comes to us, our best approach is to deny it early. If we entertain it, it will grow and overwhelm us.

This past year I noticed something in the fine print of the sports magazine that has the swimsuit issue. It read, "If you would *not* like to receive the swimsuit issue, please call this toll-free number and it will not be delivered to you. In doing so, your subscription will also be extended by one issue." So I picked up the phone and canceled it. I put that sin to death. Now I don't even have to walk it to the trash, which saves me a few steps.

LIVING INTO THE TRUTH

Think about a sin that is consistently troubling to you. Perhaps it is gossip or anger or greed. Then think about the occasions in which you most frequently face this temptation. In light of what has been said above, think about ways you can simply cut sin off before it reaches you. I know of some people who put blocks on their computers and others who have learned to avoid certain people or places that become obstacles to their life with God. Make a decision ahead of time not to engage the temptation, and walk freely from it.

AFFIRMATION

If I set my mind on the things of God, the things of earth grow strangely dim, which allows me to cut off sin the moment I encounter it. Sin can only overcome me if I enter into dialogue with it. Today I will not even think about it.

PRAYER

Lord, help me to see the areas in which my old self and its habits need to be put to death, and give me the strength and courage to do it even before it arises.

REFLECTION

What are some of the culturally acceptable forms of sin that we allow in our lives?

How could we avoid those temptations?

BODIES

*Mortify therefore your members [**bodies**]
which are upon the earth.*

<small>COLOSSIANS 3:5 (KJV)</small>

*O*ur bodies are really smart. Through habits we develop over time, they actually run our lives without our conscious effort. Though this is good, it can also be bad. If our bodies learn destructive habits, those habits can be hard to break. Fortunately, our bodies have a wonderful capacity to learn new information.

Remember when you first learned how to drive? Your hands and feet and eyes were overwhelmed: how hard do I push and turn, when do I push and turn, which is the brake and which is the gas pedal? Your body did not yet know how to operate the turn signal and keep driving at the same time. Your fingers gripped the wheel, mostly out of fear, as your heart raced and your eyes moved from windshield to mirror to pedal and back. But after a few months your body had learned how to do all of those things without you even thinking about them. Your body is intelligent; it now knows how to drive all on its own, with very little conscious effort on your part. It is the same with brushing your teeth or writing your signature.

Modern theorists agree: "Biological evidence suggests that memory resides in the whole body, such as in nerve connections and in the cells of the immune system," notes Meredith B. McGuire. But in addition to all the helpful things our bodies learn, our bodies have sin in their memories. We must help them forget these old sinful memories and develop new ones. As those in whom Christ dwells, we need to train our bodies, which are highly pliable and malleable.

Dallas Willard was once asked by a student, "How do we deal with the lust that is in our hearts?" He answered, "It is not only in our hearts, but in our bodies, particularly our eyes. We have trained them to look with the intent to gratify lust." I had never heard this idea. I asked Dallas during the break, "Do you mean to say that sin is actually in . . . my eyes, my actual eyeballs?" He said, "Yes." We often think that sin is a spiritual act, but according to Dallas, it involves bodily habits. I have come to believe he is right. When we gossip or lie, we are training our tongue to speak ill of others or not to tell the truth. The more we do it, the more naturally our tongue begins to gossip or lie, with little resistance from us. Just like driving, we have trained it to do so without our thinking.

There is good news, however. We can retrain our bodies and their natural habits. In Colossians 3:5, Paul tells us to put to death the sin that is in our "members," or our body parts. This may seem odd, but given what has been said about our bodies and knowledge, it makes sense. Our bodies have learned how to sin. They can also learn how to be virtuous.

When I was fifteen I broke a small bone in my left hand and had to have it put in a splint that was tightly taped. The problem was that I was only six weeks from starting basketball practice, and to make matters worse, I am left-handed. I was not ambidextrous in any way but fully, dominantly, left-handed. As such, I had always dribbled and shot with only my left hand (just as I always wrote, ate and brushed my teeth with my left hand). I wanted to play so badly that I went to the gym only able to use my right hand.

Every day, all by myself, I practiced dribbling. It was pretty awful at first. I bounced the ball off my foot several times and struggled to get the right rhythm. I dribbled it either too hard or too soft and was unable to maneuver well because I couldn't control the ball as easily, as naturally as I could with my left hand. Each day I practiced dribbling in and out of orange cones, going back and forth, fast and slow, left and right. I probably dribbled the ball five thousand times with my right hand, something I had never done before.

Five weeks later the x-rays showed the bone had healed in my left hand, and I was cleared to play again using both hands. A week later practice started. At the end of practice we had a scrimmage. All of my teammates knew I was dominantly left-handed and thus always dribbled to my left, which they cut off by standing to my left. On the first play I caught the ball, faked left and took off to my right, dribbling with my right hand, and shot a jump shot that swished in. Just then the coach blew his whistle. "Smith," he yelled, "come here." I did, and then he said to me privately, "When did you learn to go to your right?" I said, "Well, I broke my left hand a month ago and so for the last thirty days I have been using only my right hand when I practice. Now I guess I can use either hand."

OUR BODIES CAN BE OUR ALLY IN THE SPIRITUAL LIFE

Just as I trained my right hand to do something it had not done, so we can train our bodily members to behave as Christ-followers should behave. We can train our eyes to see beauty and to turn away from lust. We can train our tongues to tell the truth, to bless others with our words and to refrain from speaking ill of others. We can train our hands to serve others. We can train our feet to go to the least and the lost. Our bodies will not naturally be inclined this way, just as my right hand dribbled the ball off my foot for the first few weeks. But eventually it began to control the ball even without my conscious effort. That is what we are aiming for: doing the right things over and over, under the leading of the Spirit, until our bodies naturally do what is right.

So I encourage you to give thanks for your body. It is good. Then I would encourage you to think of the ways in which your body has been trained under the ideas and ideals of the kingdom of this world, and prayerfully consider how it can be retrained to be your ally in your walk in the Spirit.

LIVING INTO THE TRUTH

Think of one way you can change a bodily habit and begin practicing using your body in the way it was meant to be used.

AFFIRMATION

My body is a glorious gift from God, and I refuse to use it for sin. Instead I will celebrate it each day and train it so it becomes my ally in my apprenticeship to Jesus.

PRAYER

Abba, forgive me for not respecting the role of my body in my life with you. Thank you for this beautiful, living temple of the Spirit you have given me. Help me to purge harmful habits and start healthy ones today. Amen.

REFLECTION

How have you thought about your body as an enemy or ally in your life with God?

DESIRES

*Put to death, therefore, whatever belongs to
your earthly nature: sexual immorality, impurity, lust,
evil* **desires** *and greed, which is idolatry.*

COLOSSIANS 3:5

One night during Girl Scout cookie season (the month or two when our house is full of boxes of cookies), my daughter, Hope, came downstairs to watch a television show we both enjoy. She was holding a box of Thin Mints and was just staring at it, with a forlorn look on her face. I said, "What's the matter, Hope?"

"Dad," she said, "I just know that if I open this box I will have to eat a whole sleeve of cookies."

"You have to?" I asked.

"Yes, that is what I do every time," she said.

Coincidentally, I had been thinking over the past several weeks about our desires and how they get their grip on us, and how we can overcome their dominion. So I said, "Let me offer another idea. What if you decided to eat three, maybe four, cookies? And what if you ate them slowly and really savored each one? Do you think you could give that a try?" She looked puzzled about this odd idea.

I looked over at her about ten minutes later, and she had eaten only two cookies. She was now engrossed in the television program. About forty minutes later she said, "I'm tired, Dad. I am going to get ready for bed," and off she went. I looked over at the cookies—nearly a full sleeve left on the table—and I thought about how desires work in our lives. The act of eating slowly had taken the power out of the desire.

Desires expand when we give them a place in our lives that they do not deserve.

God created us with the capacity to desire. Can you imagine what life would be like if you suddenly lost your ability to desire anything? It would make life unbearable. Many of our desires are, in fact, very good. I desire God. I desire to live. I desire to be with my lovely wife. I desire to be a good father. Some of my desires, however, are wrong and sinful. I sometimes desire to be admired and praised. I sometimes desire to see others fail, especially people who do not like me. I sometimes desire to be rich because I could buy all the things I think would make me happy.

Even our good desires become sinful when they become all-consuming. That is the case of the sins on Paul's list in Colossians 3:5. Sexual desire is, in itself, a very good thing, created by God and an important dimension of the human person. But when it becomes dominant, it becomes deadly. Paul does not say, "Put to death sexual desire"; he says, "Put to death sexual *immorality*." He does not say, "Put to death money"; he says, "Put to death greed." Greed is an inordinate desire for money. It is wanting more and more of it, never being satisfied, to the point of even worshiping money, which is why Paul says greed is actually idolatry.

Many of our sins are the result of *disordered natural desires*. The desire for food is natural and good (if not, why did God give us taste buds?), but when it becomes our primary focus it becomes gluttony. Cookies, in moderation, can be a blessing. The need to eat an entire box of cookies is clearly the result of a good desire gone bad. The desire to feel affirmation for who we are and what we do is natural and good (think of a child beaming with joy as her parents praise her artwork and put it on the refrigerator), but when it is a constant need it becomes pride and vainglory. The desire for a glass of wine is a natural and good thing (Jesus' first miracle was to make very good wine), but when we drink too much it leads to drunkenness.

So what makes the difference? What makes sexuality *immoral*? When does the desire to have material possessions become *greed*? Desire becomes sin when it moves from being something we enjoy to something we seek as our main desire. This is the key.

When our deepest desire is for God, all other desires take their natural place. We can then enjoy things properly, with appreciation and moderation. But when God is not the center of what we do, then we must fill that void with something (cookies or cars), and when we do, we find that the desire is insatiable. The cookies cannot fill the void. So we eat more and more and feel less and less satisfied.

How do we find true delight? The same way the Trinity does. Once again, we return to Colossians 3:1-4 where Paul reveals the secret to true delight. It is the love story our hearts and souls yearn for. God, the one who created the universe, so loved us that he sent his Son, whose broken body and shed blood has reconciled us to God. And the Son rose from the dead, defeated death and imparted his eternal life to us. This sacred romance is the source of our delight. We find delight when we turn to God, with our hearts fully exposed to God's loving gaze, surrendered and content in the arms of our Father.

We are all new people, people in whom Christ dwells and delights. We are temples of the Spirit, sacred and precious. Sin sullies us. That is why Paul says, "Put it to death." He is not counseling us to put an end to all desires; rather, he is saying, "You are Christ-inhabited, fully loved and cared for. Don't seek solace in some earthly desire. Keep them in their place. Enjoy your life, just don't try to find your life in your joys." This perspective brings order to our desires. Food becomes something to be thankful for and enjoy, sexuality becomes a way to enhance intimacy with our marriage partner, and money becomes something we use to buy the things we need.

Spiritual theologian James Houston writes: "The more our desires are directed toward God, the more he transforms them, so that we desire him ever more ardently; we are changed in the very process of desiring, to desire it in an ever more godly way." We were made to desire—to desire God. As we express our longing for God, God meets us, and our heart finds what it is looking for. All of our other desires are consequently transformed. They are seen for what they are (things to be enjoyed), not invested in for what they are not (things to find our ultimate meaning in).

A few weeks after my conversation about Thin Mints with Hope, she said, "Dad, I didn't take your advice yesterday. I opened the box [of Thin Mints] and ate a whole sleeve of cookies."

"Did you enjoy them?" I asked.

"Yeah, but the rest of the day I didn't feel so good. I don't think I'll do that again. I liked having three or four better," she said.

Desires are not bad. It is only when we try to fill a void that desires destroy us.

LIVING INTO THE TRUTH

Moderation is a great thing to strive for, but seeking it in itself rarely works. The problem is that desire, if it has become inordinate, does not easily yield to a philosophical notion such as moderation. The way to reordering our desires is to find our joy in God. Today, or this week, set aside time to be in God's presence. Try to expose your heart to God, as a tulip does with the sun, opening its petals and letting the rays pour into its core. Perhaps one of the following short prayers might aid you:

"Abba, I open all of the secret places of my heart to you."

"Search me, O God, and see me as I am."

"Let me feel your love today as never before."

Then, just sit and listen for what God wants to bring to mind.

AFFIRMATION
Desire in itself is not a bad thing, but a gift from God, a part of how I was made. But pure delight, delight in God, is what I was made for. That alone can reorder the desires of my heart.

PRAYER
Gracious Abba, help me to find the hunger of my heart and soul in you and not in some earthly thing. Teach me how to enjoy the good things of this world in their proper order. Amen.

REFLECTION
What is one craving or desire you find it hard to say "enough" to?

WRATH

Because of these, the **wrath** *of God is coming.*

COLOSSIANS 3:6

I read our local newspaper this morning and found it so depressing. It was full of stories of murder, arson, theft, assault and immorality. There were several outrageous stories about celebrities and their misbehavior: adultery, sex outside of marriage, lavish spending on themselves. It was really sad. I am throwing no stones, as I am not free from sinning myself, but I wondered, *What does God feel when confronted with these reckless deeds?* According to the Bible, the answer is clear: wrath.

In Colossians 3:6, we run across the theologically volatile phrase *the wrath of God* (see also Romans 1:18; 1 Thessalo-

nians 2:16; Revelation 15:7; 19:15). We usually use the word
wrath to describe intense anger—not just normal anger, but
explosive anger, a raging anger that inflicts punishment. The
difficulty comes when we try to impose this intense kind of
anger on God. Is God sitting up in the heavens glaring down
at the people on earth, filled with rage? Many people have
that exact image of God. They are certain that God cannot
stand them and would squash them like a bug with righteous
indignation. And they are rightly afraid of this God.

How does this understanding of God mesh with the big
story of the gospel contained in the most famous of all verses:
"For God so *loved* the world that he gave his one and only Son,
that whoever believes in him shall not perish but have eternal
life. For God did not send his Son into the world to condemn
the world, but to save the world through him" (John 3:16-
17)? God so loved the world, it says. God died to save us, it
reads. God did not take on our flesh to condemn us, it pro-
claims. And yet, a little later in that same chapter in John we
have this verse: "Whoever believes in the Son has eternal life,
but whoever rejects the Son will not see life, for God's *wrath*
remains on them" (John 3:36).

We have two phrases difficult to reconcile: "the love of God"
and "the wrath of God." Unless we find a way to understand
how both can be true of God, we end up with a Jekyll and
Hyde kind of God. Many of us think God is up in heaven
chewing antacids just to keep himself from getting sick about
our sin. And yet I do not believe that God's wrath is the same

as human anger. We get angry when we don't get our way, and we scowl and stew and sometimes take it out on someone or something. That is not the kind of anger that God expresses.

God set up an order, a good order, and if we rebel from that order, we suffer. That is what the wrath of God is. Wrath is not God's disposition toward us; *wrath is God's arrangement regarding sin.* Can you imagine if sin carried no consequence? We think of sin as something that is good for us but that unfortunately makes God mad at us. We don't see sin as deadly. Yet sin is a rejection of God that takes many forms, and it naturally carries with it some kind of punishment. God isn't in the punishment business on a day-to-day, moment-to-moment basis, like some divine karma. Sin is its own punishment. Paul listed a number of sins in Colossians 3:5 (sexual immorality, impurity, lust, greed), and in 3:6 he says, "Because of these the wrath of God is coming." We assume this means that God is keeping track of every infraction and is poised to punish us for each and every one.

That is not how it works. As New Testament scholar F. F. Bruce puts it, we experience the "inevitable consequences" of our own free choice. Living in a condition of sin, in rebellion to God, cannot bring anything but sadness in our lives. Holiness is written, as Dr. Bruce says, in our "conscience and constitution," in the very fibers of our being.

God set up an order, and if we rebel from that order we suffer. That is what the wrath of God is. The order, though, is good. Can you imagine if sin carried no consequence? Sadly, most Christians do not think of God's wrath in this way. Again, they think sin is something that is pleasurable for us, but unfortunately makes God mad at us. They don't see that sin is deadly.

God is for us—that is why he hates sin. God does not need to watch us like Big Brother and exact punishment for every sin. In fact, God does not need to punish for any sin. Sin brings with it the wrath of its own punishment. You remember the old sermon title "Sinners in the Hands of an Angry God"? As Dallas Willard has said, it is actually the reverse in our churches today. It is "God in the Hands of Angry Sinners." We are the ones who impose this false image upon God.

God is love. God's disposition toward us is, and forever remains, love. If we reject that love and go our own way we feel a void that we will try to fill with the pleasures of sin. When we do that, we must expect the sad consequences. Like death and taxes, no one has been able to avoid them. *The natural consequence of sin is the wrath of our loving God.* God set up this order because he loves us. The emptiness found in sin is often the only way people will, like the prodigal son, come to their right minds and come home.

My biggest concern is not that God expresses wrath toward sin but that I too easily do not. I notice myself becoming jaded by the sin that surrounds me, and even the sin that resides within me. The headlines in the paper this morning made me feel depressed, but I wish they had made me feel something more, something like wrath. God's people are being harmed by one another, and that alone ought to cause me to feel the same wrath that God feels. Perhaps a good place to begin is to ask God to help us see sin as he does, as nothing more than a force of destruction, and to learn how to shun it for that very reason. That is a prayer I suspect God will answer.

LIVING INTO THE TRUTH

Using a journal or notebook, write out a list of sins and then describe the natural consequences of those sins. You can use the classic seven deadly sins of pride, envy, anger, sloth, greed, gluttony and lust. For example:

> *Envy.* Natural consequences: unhappiness with life; anger toward others who have something we do not; lack of appreciation for what we have; despair; plotting for gain

As you write the consequences out, pay attention to the consistency, and thus the unavoidability, of the consequences.

AFFIRMATION

God has ordered this world so that sin will naturally harm me. This is not because God is mean, but because God loves me. I am therefore thankful for the wrath of God toward sin.

PRAYER

Gracious Abba, I find sin tempting, and I find myself jaded at times. But you are teaching me that sin has natural and unavoidable consequences. Help me not only to tire of sin but to hate it as you do. Teach me how to say no to it and yes to you, which is my only hope of a good and beautiful life. Amen.

REFLECTION

How does this idea that the wrath of God is the attitude of God toward sin (and not toward us) help us love him even more?

- 13 -

WALK

*You used to **walk** in these ways.*

Colossians 3:7

Several years ago I went back to my hometown. One day during that visit I walked around a huge shopping mall. Suddenly I heard a voice from my past: "Smith—how's it going?" It was my high school track coach and his wife. "Looks like you've lost a little hair," he said with a smile, "but I can tell you this—you have exactly the same gait you had in high school. I saw you across the mall, probably a hundred yards away, and I saw you walking and I said to my wife, 'Honey, that's Jim Smith.' She said, 'How do you know that—he's so far away and you haven't seen him in years?' I said, 'He has the exact same walk as Smith. It's got to be him.' Though he knew me well, I was amazed that he could recognize me simply by observing my walk from a distance both in time and space.

The word *walk* is used throughout the Bible as a kind of metaphor for how a person lives: "And now, Israel, what does the LORD your God ask of you but to fear the LORD your God, to *walk* in obedience to him, to love him, to serve the LORD your God with all your heart and with all your soul" (Deuteronomy 10:12). According to one biblical scholar, the word *walk* was used to describe a "participation in a course of life." The way we walk refers to the way we go about our lives, the things we do daily, the way we think and act, activities that make up the routine of our lives. In verse 7 Paul is telling the Colossians that before they became united with Jesus in his death and resurrection, they walked a certain way, one that was characterized by sin: "You used to walk in these ways" he reminds them, "in the life you once lived."

The way God calls us to walk has to do with light and truth and love. Jesus said, "I am the light of the world. Whoever follows me will never walk in darkness, but will have the *light* of life" (John 8:12). Have you ever tried to walk in the dark? It is slow and scary. Jesus said those who follow him—who live as his apprentice, doing what he did and thinking what he thought—will never walk in darkness because he is the light of the world. He lit this world up with the reality that at the heart of the universe is a beautiful, loving power. When we learn to see the world by the light of

Christ, the whole world looks different, luminous. Then we can see things as they are. We can see where we are. We can see *who* we are.

Each day as we get out of bed we face a world that tells us that we are alone, that we are what we accomplish and that certain doom is around the corner. One of the things light does is reveal the truth. Jesus' disciple John wrote, "It gave me great joy when some believers came and testified about your faithfulness to the truth, telling how you continue to walk in it" (3 John 3). Thanks to Jesus I know who I am (Jim in whom Christ dwells) and I know where I live (in the strong and unshakeable kingdom of God). I love walking in the light. And this is not "pie in the sky" wishful thinking. This is true.

We walk in the light, and we know the truth. The primary truth we learn in this walk with Jesus is that we are loved. The apostle John also wrote, "And this is love: that we walk in obedience to his commands. As you have heard from the beginning, his command is that you walk in *love*" (2 John 6). In Jesus we can now walk in the light, but more than that, when we walk in obedience to his commands we naturally walk in love. That reality is illumined by the life of Jesus. The incarnation, death and resurrection of Jesus is a declaration of love. When we reflect on the lowly manger and the blood-stained cross and the empty tomb we know one thing for sure: we are loved. "This is love: not that we loved God, but that he loved us and sent his Son as an atoning sacrifice for our sins" (1 John 4:10). And because we are loved, so we love: "Dear friends, since God so loved us, we also ought to love one another" (1 John 4:11).

There is so much darkness, so much falsehood and so much hatred in this world. That is what so many people are walking in. But Jesus comes and teaches us how to walk in another way. Walking with Jesus helps us know that we are not alone, that we are sacred beings of immense worth regardless of what we do, and that great joy awaits us. We walk with Jesus and therefore we walk in the light, because he *is* the light. We walk with Jesus and therefore we walk in the truth, because he is the truth. We walk with Jesus and therefore we walk in love, because he is love.

For a time in my life, before I chose to be an apprentice of Jesus, I walked in darkness, deception and depravity. I no longer walk in those ways. The light went on, the truth appeared, and the love came in. I now walk differently, thanks to Jesus. My steps are more sure because I know who I am and where I am going.

Jesus' words are true. They are "a lamp unto my feet, and a light unto my path" (Psalm 119:105 KJV). Now I walk in his teachings, and I am walking in the truth. My steps are guided by compassion. As one who is deeply loved, so I am called to love, and my feet now take me to those who are in need of a kind word or a simple presence. I am walking in love, and thus walking for love.

I cannot say that my old ways of walking are entirely

behind me. If you are like me, you have times when you avoid the light, the truth and the love that Jesus has given us. The good news is that he never gives up on us. He never stops shining; he remains the truth, and his love never fails.

LIVING INTO THE TRUTH

Today, or this week, reflect on one of the three gifts Jesus offers us: light, truth and love. Pick one and focus on what it means to walk in that gift. Write in your journal about the blessing that gift is. For example, to know that we are walking in the truth means that Jesus' teachings are absolutely true and reliable. To know that we are walking in the light means that Jesus' teachings make everything clear and we are thus able to see where we are going. To know that we are walking in love means that we will never take a single step without the assurance that God is smiling on us, and perhaps that will help us smile at those around us.

AFFIRMATION

The light, truth and love of Jesus are gifts given to me. I do not deserve them. I did not create them. I cannot lose them. I can only walk in them, and when I do, the whole world will know I am his apprentice.

PRAYER

Gracious Abba, thank you for sending your Son, Jesus, who is the light of the world, the truth and the love that I need.

Help me to know and appreciate this gift, and help me to walk in it all the days of my life. Amen.

REFLECTION

When people see you walk—your way of living—what might they conclude about you and who you follow?

ONCE

*You used to walk in these ways, in the life you **once** lived.*

COLOSSIANS 3:7

When I became a Christ-follower at the age of eighteen, my life began to change. After two years of soul searching and emptiness, I finally felt a deep inner peace. The Bible, which had once been intimidating, became my treasured companion. My parents gave me a King James Bible, and I read it day and night. I began praying regularly and writing in a journal. After years of liking church in the same way I liked going to the dentist, I wanted—*wanted*—to go to church. Something was alive and growing inside of me. Unfortunately, my birth from above did not eradicate sin in my life. The years I had spent learning how to lie and lust, to cuss and to get angry, were still very much in my "members," woven into the very fibers of my being.

During my first semester of college (at a school known as a "party school") I lived in a co-ed dorm. There were girls living on my floor? Whoa. Two weeks into the semester our floor hosted a "Boxer-Hawaiian" party, which meant people— guys *and* girls—were to wear Hawaiian shirts and boxer shorts. There were also three kegs of beer. The next morning I felt terrible. Though I didn't commit any noteworthy sins that night, and in fact participated less and went to bed earlier than I would have in the past, I didn't feel good about it. Six months earlier I would have had no qualms about what I had done. Now I felt a deep uneasiness in my heart.

That next weekend I went home and shared my experience with a close friend, a long-time Christian who had prayed for me to come to Christ. He said, "You can't go to parties, man. If you keep doing that you will lose your salvation. In fact, I am beginning to wonder if you are really born again." I was bewildered by his reaction. I hadn't committed any great sin, and I was honestly seeking good pastoral advice—which I did not get. The next week he wrote me a letter and sent it to my dorm. In it he went even further, quoting verses in the Bible about God's wrath toward sin, and said that if I didn't repent God would punish me. The implication was clear: if I was genuinely a Christian I would never go to a party again. Oddly, his letter did not fill me with conviction, only confusion.

Making the adjustment from the ways of the world to the ways of the kingdom is hard. But guilt is a poor motivator. My friend thought keeping rules ("Don't go to parties") was the right way, and used guilt to enforce them. This was simply not helpful to me. Being an apprentice of Jesus is not about rules and laws, it is about identity and place. The Christian life is not an if-then obligation ("*If* I do this, *then* God will do that"). It is a because-therefore opportunity ("*Because* I am one in whom Christ dwells, *therefore* I will . . ."). The better way to encourage change is to remind people who they are *now* in contrast to who they *once* were. That's what Paul does in his letters to new Christians. Christ lives in us, and our life is in him. Instead of applying guilt, we should say to ourselves, *I am a Christ-inhabited person. What does that look like in the world I live in?*

There is no escaping the reality—thanks be to God—that I am one in whom Christ dwells and therefore I am called to live differently than the life I *once* lived. *Not because my salvation is dependent on it.* Not because God will be mad at me if I do not. Not even because people are watching what I do and when I sin it is a bad witness. Put simply, I am called to live differently because I am not the person I *once* was. Paul's logic is consistent in all of his epistles (see, for example, Ephesians 2 and Romans 5–6). It is not a matter of salvation; it is a matter of being authentically who we are.

I *once* lied because I thought it helped me get what I want. In truth, it made me feel ashamed and it fractured relationships. Now I tell the truth because God provides what I need, and I respect people and value my relationships enough not to lie to them.

I *once* overindulged with food and drink because it numbed my pain and made me feel alive. It also made me feel dead inside, and in the morning the pain was more acute. Now I enjoy all things in moderation, with thanksgiving, not seeking in a bottle what I have in my soul—inner satisfaction.

I *once* used people to get what I want, *once* tried to manage their opinions of me, *once* trained my eyes to lust, *once* trained my tongue to gossip. That is a life I *once* lived. But it wasn't really living at all. It was a slow death, a gradual descent into darkness.

Now I have a new nature. It no longer needs to sin, and in fact, it cannot run on sin as it once did when it knew no better. I am different from the person I once was.

I felt bad after that party—not because going to a party is, in itself, a sin, but because I was trying to be someone I used to be but was no longer, and it felt wrong in my soul. Never again can I live as I once lived. To be sure, I continue to struggle with sin, but I see sin now as a bad choice, not merely a rule to break. I understand that it is not a matter of rule keeping, it is a matter of *being who I am*.

Since college I have been to many parties, but I know now that I never have to check my true identity at the door. Jesus once attended a wedding party, and I assume he did not stand in a corner and scowl at everyone (instead he made more wine when they ran out). I assume he laughed and enjoyed himself and enjoyed and loved all the people around him. It is possible, after all, to have a good time without sinning. And, to be honest, the only way we can genuinely have a good time is without sinning. I *once* was blind to this, but now I see.

LIVING INTO THE TRUTH

Today, or this week, focus on a life situation you face regularly—a place you go, an activity you engage in. Reflect on how your status as an apprentice of Jesus affects how you participate in it. For example, if at your workplace there is a lounge where coworkers gather, how would your identity in Christ influence your behavior among them? Or perhaps you go to a gym to exercise. How might your status as an apprentice shape how you interact with others? Try to avoid guilt as a motivator and external behavior as a goal. Think about your heart—a Christ-inhabited heart—and what that means in terms of how you approach your life.

AFFIRMATION

I am a new creature in Christ—the old has passed, the new has come. Today I will let my identity—not trying to keep rules—shape my behavior.

PRAYER

Gracious Abba, it is hard at times to shake off who I once was.

Help me to focus not on behavior but on identity. You have made me a new creation. Help me to see that and to live accordingly. Amen.

REFLECTION

If you could change one thing about your behavior, what would it be? How can your identity as one in whom Christ dwells affect that behavior?

MOUTH

But now you must get rid of all such things—
anger, wrath, malice, slander, and abusive
language from your **mouth.**

COLOSSIANS 3:8 (NRSV)

What we say to one another can cause a great deal of harm. In his epistle, James says:

> The *tongue* is a small part of the body, but it makes great boasts. Consider what a great forest is set on fire by a small spark. The *tongue* also is a fire, a world of evil among the parts of the body. It corrupts the whole body, sets the whole course of one's life on fire, and is itself set on fire by hell. . . . No human being can tame the *tongue.*

It is a restless evil, full of deadly poison. With the *tongue* we praise our Lord and Father, and with it we curse human beings, who have been made in God's likeness. (James 3:5-6, 8-9)

In Colossians 3:8-9, Paul tells us to get rid of "abusive language" from our mouths. The NIV reads "filthy language from your lips," but this is easily misunderstood as referring to cursing, or using "dirty words" or expletives. The Greek word Paul uses refers to the kind of abusive language we use when we want to hurt someone with our words. There are many people who never curse but who use their lips to say mean and spiteful things to others that cause a lot of hurt. That is what Paul is telling us to get rid of.

When we are hurt by someone, we usually want to hurt back. It seems to take away the pain, at least for a moment. Most of us do not resort to physical violence; instead, we use our words to hurt others. Sometimes it is simply saying something bad about someone without them being present, such as gossip. But at other times we say things directly to others with the intent of hurting their feelings, which is what Paul is addressing in Colossians 3. Anger, rage and malice nearly always come out in slander or abusive language.

But you and I have a new way to deal with our hurts. We are precious children of God who live in the safety and security of our Father's kingdom. We are heirs with Jesus who await a certain and blessed future. What others may say and do cannot thwart this reality. So we can refrain from using our mouths and lips to harm those who harm us. We can choose, instead, to use our gift of speech to bless those who would curse us. That is exactly what Jesus called us to do, and as his apprentices, we can learn to do this.

A close friend of mine was caught in a difficult and painful legal matter. He was being sued by someone, and he was clearly innocent. I walked with him through this difficult time as the opposing lawyers tried to slander him, accusing him of things he did not do. In the end, justice prevailed, and he was acquitted of all of the charges brought against him. The amazing thing about this experience for me was watching how he, as a Christ-follower, refrained from speaking ill of his accuser. He was calm and polite in an extremely trying situation. His deep awareness of his identity in Christ and his place in the kingdom—coupled with the certainty of his innocence—allowed him to hold his tongue.

His example stays with me as I face much lesser threats. In a given week I might encounter people who disagree with me or perhaps even challenge me. Or I might be confronted by someone who openly criticizes me. This is a natural part of life when humans interact. Each of these are opportunities for me to remember who I am and where I live. I try to live each day with the awareness that my tongue can do a lot of damage, but also with the awareness that my words can heal and bless others.

One week I set a goal to use my words to bless someone

once each day. It was an easy and enjoyable exercise. As I interacted with people I began to look for the good in who they were or in what they were doing. I would take a moment to compose a blessing or to find a way to let them know how much I appreciated what they had done. Each time I delivered this kind of benediction (which literally means "good word") to that chosen person I watched as their countenance was uplifted. A smile invariably came over their face.

God gave us mouths and tongues to comfort and encourage one another. In that sense, we participate with the work of the Holy Spirit. Jesus called the Spirit the "paraclete" (John 14:26), which means comforter or advocate. The Spirit comes to me daily with a word of inspiration, always reminding me who I am and whose I am. We have that same opportunity. As apprentices of Jesus we must not set the bar merely at not harming others with our speech, but with using our words to uplift and console, to encourage and to bless.

One practice I enjoy is to ask God to bring me someone each day for whom my words can be a blessing. God is faithful in answering this prayer. I try to keep the eyes of my heart open to see who that person might be and then to pay attention to the nudge of the Spirit when I come into their presence. Not long ago I did this, and the person I encouraged later sent me a text that said, "You will never know how much your kind words meant to me. I was really struggling that day, and I did not let anyone know. My faith was sagging, and my soul was hurting, when suddenly you said those words that changed everything. Thank you."

It is a delight to use our mouths to bring God glory.

LIVING INTO THE TRUTH

Today, or this week, pay attention to your lips, to your tongue, to the things you say. Consciously use them to bless people. Make it a goal to say ten kind and encouraging things to those around you on any given day. Also try to go a day without gossiping. If you slip up and secretly slander someone by gossiping, first ask God to change your heart toward that person. Second, begin praying for them and their well-being and success. Third, send them a note of encouragement.

AFFIRMATION

The tongue is a mighty force that can harm or heal. Under the leadership of Jesus, I can tame my tongue and train it to be used to bless and not to curse.

PRAYER

Gracious Abba, my lips are not yet sanctified. Anger and resentment find their way into my words. Help me to see others as you see them, as children made in your image. Teach me how to use words to bring light and life to those around me. Amen.

REFLECTION

What recent examples of how you have spoken in a hurtful way toward or in a slanderous way about others come to mind? Confess them to the Lord knowing that he offers you grace and a chance to begin again.

16

CLOTHES

*You have stripped off the old self with its practices
and have **clothed** yourselves with the new self.*

COLOSSIANS 3:9-10 (NRSV)

On the day of my wedding, my groomsmen and I played a game of touch football. Knowing that we would all end up getting pretty dirty, we put on old T-shirts, shorts and beat-up tennis shoes. Sure enough, by the end of the game we were sweaty, covered in dirt and mud, with grass stains on our shirts, shorts and socks. We looked gross and grimy. We then went back to the hotel, where some of the bridesmaids saw us. They were dressed beautifully, with their hair and make-up professionally done. "You boys better start getting ready," one of them said. Within an hour we were back in the lobby, looking spotless and dapper in our tuxedos. "Wow," the same bridesmaid said, "you guys clean up pretty nice."

Just as my guys and I stripped out of our dirty athletic clothes, scrubbed down and then put on our finest apparel, so also we who are apprentices of Jesus must take off our old clothes and put on new ones. In Colossians 3:9-10, clothes are a metaphor for behavior: some we must take off, and others we must put on.

In the previous chapters of this book we have been looking at some of the "old clothes" we need to throw into the trash: the apparel of anger, lust and lying, the garb of malice, greed and immorality. We used to wear those clothes before we became people in whom Christ dwells and delights. They were our natural wardrobe. Without Christ living in us, enlivening us, making us new, we were spiritually dead, alone and scared. We put on anger in order to manage others; we put on lust in order to feel intimacy; we put on deception in order to get what we wanted. Even though they were filthy rags, they were all we had.

But now we are Christ-inhabited. We live in the strong and unshakable kingdom of God. We know who we are and whose we are. We know where we live now, and where we will dwell forever. The old clothes simply must go. We don't need anger, lust and lying; we have no need for rage, slander and greed. So, just as my groomsmen and I did on our wedding day, we strip off the filthy clothes. And in their place we put on our very best attire. Over the next several verses in

Colossians 3 (especially verse 12) Paul will tell us what kinds of clothing we are to put on.

Apprentices of Jesus put on *compassion.* Christ-followers wear *kindness* each day. Students of Jesus put on *humility* and *gentleness* and *patience.* These are the clothes we now wear. Not because Jesus said we must. Not because we risk losing our salvation. But because those are the only clothes fit for children of the King. We are royalty. Those virtues are the clothes we wear because Christ has made us virtuous. The image Paul gives us of having stripped off old filthy rags and put on new clothes begins the transition from getting rid of vices to putting on virtues. Christians—by virtue of the life of Jesus now in them—discard their former sinful practices like old, ill-fitting clothes and don the apparel that reflects our new nature: compassion, kindness, humility, gentleness and patience.

In the morning I often stop and think about what to wear that day. I consider the weather—will it be hot, cold or mild? Then I think about what I will be doing that day—do I have meetings where certain attire is expected? Most of us have, at one time or another, tried to "dress to impress." It is nice to hear people say, "I like that shirt. It looks good on you." But lately, thanks to Colossians 3:9-10, I pause each day and go over my list of five items that Christ-followers are privileged to wear. I think about these virtues, how I have been given them and how I might let others see them on me that day.

I think about putting on compassion. The Trinity is full

of compassion toward me, and toward all people. Compassion entails a sympathetic understanding of the condition of another. I think about the people I will meet today. Will I judge them, or will I strive to understand them, to be aware that they are fighting a great battle, as we all are? I resolve to put on compassion, and gently slip it on.

I then think about kindness. There is so little of it in our world today. But Jesus is my master teacher, and like him, I will show kindness today. I will try to open doors for people, let them in my lane while driving, smile at people and speak encouraging words.

Next I think about humility. Humility is not the same as having a bad, or low, opinion of ourselves. Rather, humility is thinking rightly about ourselves, and the truth about me is that by myself I am weak and sinful. I have nothing to boast about. If I have done anything worthy, it is because of God at work in me. I resolve to put on humility this day by not thinking highly of myself and, instead, thinking highly of others.

I think about gentleness. One can only be gentle if one is strong; the weak cannot be gentle. I am strong because of where I live (the kingdom) and because of who I am (Jim in whom Christ dwells and delights). I decide that I will not use that strength this day to be aggressive, but rather to be gentle. People need the quiet strength I have to offer, thanks to the Spirit.

Finally, I think about patience. When I have amnesia about

my identity and place, forgetting who I am and where I live, I struggle with impatience. I want things when I want them, and do not like to wait. But today I will remember who I am and who is in control. I resolve to put on patience and simply let things be as they are. When they do not go as I want them to, I will smile and turn to God and say, "Thank you for this chance to exercise patience."

New clothes fit for the new creation. We can only put these on because of what God, in Christ, has done. Our life in Christ makes compassion, kindness, humility, gentleness and patience possible. But mark this: we have to put them on; God will not put them on for us. Apprenticeship to Jesus always involves our effort. So this day we are called to put on these virtues. They are waiting in our closet. I pray you put them on. The world does not need to be impressed by our dress, but it is very much in need of genuine compassion, kindness, humility, gentleness and patience. They are rarely seen, and are the most beautiful attire anyone can wear.

LIVING INTO THE TRUTH

Today try the practice I described above. Take a few minutes to think about each of the five items of clothing: compassion, kindness, humility, gentleness and patience. Reflect on where they come from, and resolve to put them on this very day. Perhaps it might be best to take one virtue at a time for five days. One day reflect on compassion, for example, and look for ways to exhibit it on that day.

AFFIRMATION

God has cleaned me up, given me new life and also given me a new set of clothes to wear. They are a gift, but I must put them on. Today I will, for the world is badly in need of people who are compassionate, kind, humble, gentle and patient.

PRAYER

Gracious Abba, thank you for these wonderful items of apparel. I did not earn them; they are a gift from you. Help me honor you this day, as well as those around me, by putting on compassion, kindness, humility, gentleness and patience. Amen.

REFLECTION

Have you ever tried to "dress to impress" others? Did it work?

17

KNOWLEDGE

. . . the new self, which is being renewed in **knowledge.**

COLOSSIANS 3:10

Knowledge is power" the old saying goes. And it is true.

When we know something we have that knowledge at our disposal. If you know—and understand—algebra, for example, you have the power to solve mathematical problems. If you know Chinese, you have the power to speak and understand that language, which may be essential in a business deal.

I recently blew a breaker in our house, and we were without electricity for two days as I tried my best to fix the problem. I called an expert electrician who knows all about electrical wiring, and he solved the problem in less than ten minutes. Knowledge, in this case, was literally power.

There is a lot to know in this vast universe. And in this "information age" we have access to more knowledge than we can handle. My iPhone, for example, has access to more information than is stored in the entire Harvard Library. I can do a search on the Internet and within seconds have a recipe for Baked Alaska. These little screens we now possess are like portals to vast amounts of knowledge. I suspect that is why our cell phones are so addictive—they can access knowledge, which is a form of power. And we like power.

Unfortunately all of that information, all of that knowledge, is secondary. While it is useful and beneficial to know how to speak Chinese or make Baked Alaska, that knowledge is something we can live without. What is the most important knowledge we can have? Knowledge of God. Knowledge of God is the highest knowledge a human can aspire to know. If there is a God, if there really is a Creator, if there really is an almighty Deity, then knowing and understanding this God would be the supreme knowledge. Every other kind of knowledge would pale in comparison.

However, our small, finite minds cannot grasp the infinite, eternal God. Human reason is unable to comprehend God. So in order for us to know God, he will have to reveal himself to us in ways we can understand. That is precisely what God, through Jesus, has done:

All things have been committed to me by my Father. No

one knows who the Son is except the Father, and no
one knows who the Father is except the Son and those
to whom the Son chooses to *reveal* him. (Luke 10:22)

Jesus reveals the Father to us. And he does it through the
Holy Spirit:

All that belongs to the Father is mine. That is why I said
the Spirit will receive from me what he will make
known to you. (John 16:15)

How does this work? How does the Spirit make Jesus and
the Father knowable to us?

The Spirit does not lead us through a curriculum of facts
about God but rather guides us into the depths of the relationship between the Father and the Son, which is self-sacrificial
love. The light of the Spirit falls on the love between the
Father and the Son, which tells us the whole story of the
world and gives meaning to everything, especially our lives.

- The Spirit enables us to see and know God.

- The Spirit tells us that God is beautiful, good and true.

- The Spirit whispers to us that God is love, that we are
  loved.

The Spirit encourages us to set our minds on things above,
to bathe our thoughts in the life, teaching, death, resurrection
and ascension of Jesus. The Spirit witnesses to the love between the Father and the Son and invites us to participate in

that loving communion. The Spirit reveals the greatest knowledge the world has ever heard: "the mystery that has been kept hidden for ages and generations, but is now disclosed to the Lord's people" (Colossians 1:26). That mystery is the good news of the now-available life with God.

The Spirit also tells us who we are. Identity is a never-ceasing issue for most of us. We want so badly to think well of ourselves, to believe we are valued and important. But on our own all we have are opinions from others and from ourselves. We tell ourselves we are good (or bad), and we spend each day searching for some evidence to prove it, only to have to do it all over again the next day. The verdict never comes in. Our egos are always on trial. But the Spirit witnesses with our spirit, telling us we are our Abba's child, in whom he is well pleased (Romans 8:16)—not because of our performance or accomplishments, our holiness or virtue, but because we are sacred beings of invaluable worth.

How do we know this? The Spirit imparts this crucial knowledge as we dwell on the mystery now disclosed in the sacrifice of the Son. The Lamb of God willingly laid down his life for us while we were yet sinners, sinners that God desperately loved. That is what the cross means, but it is foolishness to the human mind on its own. Only by the witness of the Spirit can we grasp this incredible mystery. And when we do, it changes everything. We now know who we are: beloved children of God. Yes, still sinful, imperfect, flawed and at times downright despicable in our thoughts, words and deeds. But loved nonetheless. And forgiven forever, made holy by the Christ who dwells within us.

This is knowledge that changes everything, the most important knowledge any human can know. But it is not to be understood as a theory; it must be grasped as a living reality. It is experiential knowledge; this knowledge must be lived. And when we grasp this knowledge, we are renewed. Our lives are transformed. If knowledge is, in fact, power, then this knowledge is the most powerful reality anyone can know—not knowledge *about* God, but rather knowledge *of* God. Thanks be to God, through Jesus and the Holy Spirit we can know it.

LIVING INTO THE TRUTH

Read John 5. Before you begin, ask the Spirit to help you know and understand whatever he has in store for you. Take your time and read it slowly. As you do, think about what has been said in this chapter, namely, that Jesus reveals God to us. Enter into this powerful passage using not only your reason but also your imagination. Imagine that you are there, listening to Jesus along with those original hearers. Pay attention to each thing he tells us about God. Jesus is giving us the most important knowledge we can ever know. Soak it in, savoring each phrase. Let your mind dwell on these important truths. If you encounter some new knowledge or understanding of God, write it in your journal. Again, ask the Spirit to help you attain this knowledge not only in your mind but in your heart as well.

AFFIRMATION

The Spirit witnesses to me in whispers, revealing the amazing love between Jesus and his heavenly Father, and in so doing, witnesses to our spirit that we are his beloved children in whom God is well pleased.

PRAYER

Gracious Abba, thank you for sending your Son, Jesus, to make you known to us. And thank you for sending the Holy Spirit to lead us into these truths. Increase my knowledge of you, so that my new self can be renewed. Amen.

REFLECTION

If you could have a better knowledge of one aspect of God, what would it be?

ALL

*Here there is no Gentile or Jew,
circumcised or uncircumcised, barbarian, Scythian,
slave or free, but Christ is **all**, and is in **all**.*

COLOSSIANS 3:11

The year was AD 202. Christians were being martyred in the Roman arena as punishment for defying the law that demanded everyone in the empire worship the gods of Rome. It was also a way to keep order. No one dared defy the empire because they knew the consequences. One day, however, the spectators witnessed something unheard of. A well-known, well-to-do Roman matron named Perpetua was about to be killed. That in itself was not so strange. But Perpetua was holding the hand of a young woman named Felicitas, who was also to be martyred for her faith in Jesus. The odd part was that Felicitas had been Perpetua's slave.

In Roman society the caste system was clear. Slaves were not considered humans, but merely tools to serve the wealthy. But in Christ there is no distinction between persons. Perpetua and Felicitas were sisters in Christ. Perpetua reached out for the hand of Felicitas because, though they were different on the social scale, they were one in Christ. Both women faced the same death for the same faith. The audience could do nothing but marvel at what they witnessed that day. These two women showed the world that to be a follower of Jesus means that all lines of separation and distinction are abolished.

In verse 11 Paul tells the Colossians, "Here there is no Gentile or Jew, circumcised or uncircumcised, barbarian, Scythian, slave or free, but Christ is all, and is in all" (Colossians 3:11). What does Paul mean by "here"? He is referring to the body of Christ, the gathered community of Christians, the church. *Here,* in the church of Jesus, things are very different from *there*—the rest of the world. In the world Paul lived in, as well as the world we live in, people separate from each other on the basis of race, religion, social class, education, gender and political ideology. Very clear lines are drawn, and seldom do people cross those lines due to deep suspicion and fear. People are afraid of those who look different, think differently and act differently than them.

But all of that changes when we become people in whom Christ dwells and delights. The distinctions of race and gender, education and ideology are no longer a cause for separation. We now share a deeper bond. Paul gives us the secret to this unity in diversity: "Christ is *all,* and is in *all*." He uses the word "all" twice, each time to make a key point. First, Jesus is all. There is no one greater than Jesus. As the only-begotten Son, the Alpha and the Omega, he rules the universe. There is nothing higher, nothing more important, nothing more sacred or more valuable or truer than Jesus. So as we pledge our allegiance to King Jesus we become fellow citizens of the kingdom of God, where all people are created equal. Second, Jesus is *in* all of us. We are Christ-inhabited. His life is flowing in each of us, and that life is the bond of our unity. Jesus is in me, and Jesus is in you, so regardless of your gender, race, economic status, we are one.

A few years ago I was in a church in Brazil. Brazil has been a melting pot of different races for several generations. There are some forty-nine recognized skin tones. When I entered this Presbyterian church, I felt I was truly in a foreign land. For all that we speak about our diversity as the body of Christ, sadly, in most of our churches there is little of it. White people worship with white people, middle class with middle class, liberals with liberals, and so on. But in this church I saw something different, a reflection of the larger body of Christ. There were men and women whose appearance and economic status were widely different. Though I do not know Portuguese, the language barrier between us did not get in the way of the unity I felt with them. Once we began singing, the pastor asked us to join hands, and in that moment I felt for a moment what Paul is talking about in Colossians 3:11.

Paul does not merely say, "We are all one in Christ." In this verse and a parallel verse (Galatians 3:28), Paul actually names the five lines of division that were common in his world. The first was race: Jews and Greeks. Religion was also a dividing piont—the circumcised and the uncircumcised. A third dividing line was culture: barbarian and Scythian—two types of people who were regarded as "less than" in the Greco-Roman world, much like the way we call people "hicks" or "rednecks" today. The fourth was caste: slave and free. And the fifth line of division was gender: male and female.

Christianity gave birth to the narrative that all of humankind is essentially one. The world would never arrive at this notion. It was the incarnation, death and resurrection of Jesus—and the indwelling Christ who came as a result of that—that enabled people to see beyond skin and social class. Professor Max Mueller points out, "Humanity is a word which you look for in vain in Plato or Aristotle; the idea of mankind as one family, as the children of one God, is an idea of Christian growth."

One of the fears people have with the idea of becoming "one" is that we can lose our diversity in the name of unity. Paul never says that our distinctive *differences* must be abolished, only the sense of *status* based on those distinctives. At the end of the letter to the Colossians (4:7-15) Paul mentions his coworkers, which included a diverse group of people: a wealthy householder (Tychicus), a slave (Onesimus), a physician (Luke), and others who are both Jews and Gentiles. In Paul's eyes they are all "brothers" in Christ. He even asks the Colossians to send his regards to Nympha, a wealthy woman who offers her home for the Colossian Christians to meet in. He practiced what he preached.

When we celebrate Communion we gather as a group of different people, and as the Methodist liturgy says, "We who are many are one in Christ." When we all eat of the same bread we acknowledge our unity in diversity. It is a beautiful thing to witness, unseen anywhere else in the world. From the time of Perpetua and Felicitas to today, Chrstians have been a witness to this unity. May we continue to cause people to say of us what Tertullian reports was said of the early Christians: "See how they love one another."

LIVING INTO THE TRUTH

Today, or this week, intentionally seek to reach out to people who are different from you. Perhaps you might want to shop in a different part of town or worship at a church whose members are a different ethnicity or social class than you. Use Paul's phrase as much as you can: "Christ is all, and is in all."

AFFIRMATION

In Christ we are all one. Regardless of our outer differences, our inner sameness gives us unity in our diversity, which is just as God designed us to be.

PRAYER

Gracious Abba, you made a beautiful and diverse world of people, but we confess that too often we shrink back in fear of people who are different from us. Give us the eyes you have, which see all people as one, especially those who call you Lord. Amen.

REFLECTION

If people looked at your close friends, would they see more similarity or more difference from you?

19

CHOSEN

*Therefore, as God's **chosen** people, holy
and dearly loved, clothe yourselves with compassion,
kindness, humility, gentleness and patience.*

COLOSSIANS 3:12

My friends Tim and Lori Gillach were living a good and satisfying life. They had two children, ages nine and eleven, and were active in their church. One evening Tim said to Lori, "Why do you think we were put on this earth? What is it that we are uniquely called to do?" They both agreed that it was to be parents. (As an onlooker I can tell you that they are extraordinary parents.)

Lori then asked, "Do you think we should have another child?" Because of their age they both knew that this would involve adoption. They prayed, and both felt it was the right thing to do. Lori began doing research and learned that baby girls in China were being abandoned to orphanages in large numbers. So they put in all of their paperwork and waited.

A few months later they were informed they had been selected to become the parents of a little girl in a remote part of China. Lori and a friend took a long and arduous journey—planes, trains and buses—that took several days, in order to reach the little girl they would name Chloe. Little Chloe's head was shaven because of lice, and her living conditions were sparse. Lori took her in her arms, and they began the journey home. When they arrived back in the U.S. they were greeted at the airport by Tim and their other two children, who held signs that said, "Welcome home, Chloe."

It is safe to say that Chloe's life drastically changed. She had been living a meager existence, with no mother or father, and with little hope for a good future. Now she lives in a beautiful home with two loving parents, two doting siblings and a very bright future.

I thought of Chloe one day when I was reading Colossians 1 and came across these verses:

> . . . giving joyful thanks to the Father, who has qualified you to share in the inheritance of his holy people in the kingdom of light. For he has rescued us from the dominion of darkness and brought us into the kingdom of the Son he loves. (Colossians 1:12-13)

Tim and Lori had welcomed Chloe into the Gillach family. She bears the family name and shares in the inheritance of that family. She was "rescued" from a dire situation and brought into a realm of plenty.

In Colossians 3:12 Paul tells the Colossians that they are "God's *chosen* people, holy and dearly loved." The concept of being chosen by God goes back to the Israelites, whom God chose to be his people. But in the new covenant, God has chosen people outside of Israel to be his people, as we saw in the previous chapter. Now both Jew and Greek, barbarian, Scythian, slave and free are members of God's household, chosen and adopted and brought into the family. Notice the two adjectives that follow "chosen": *holy* and *dearly loved*. These two words describe the nature of those whom God has chosen and adopted.

First, they are "holy." We must be careful not to assume that the Colossians (or us, for that matter) are holy in terms of their behavior. The word *holy* refers to that which is sacred and special and which should be cared for because it is sacred and special. Think of some family heirloom you have. It may be of little value to anyone else, but to you it is sacred, and you treat it that way. We are people in whom Christ dwells and are therefore sacred, holy and special. We are holy because God has chosen us. And, of course, our behavior ought to reflect that as well. Just as we would never throw our family heirloom in the mud, so also we ought to walk in holiness.

Second, those God has chosen are "dearly loved." Do you know how much God loves you? It is beyond your imagination. God loved you into existence and has given you life and breath and grace and sustenance all of your days. Jesus willingly went to the cross to demonstrate his love to you (Romans 5:8). You are not merely someone God *likes* (though he does); you are someone God *loves*. It is the work of the Holy Spirit to tell you that eternal love has chosen you—not merely all people, but *you*. You did not merit this love, and therefore you cannot lose it. Just as you are holy and your character should naturally reflect that, so also the fact that you are dearly loved should naturally be shown in your love for God and for others.

Watching Chloe grow up has been a joy. She is now a happy, vibrant, loving young woman. She loves her family, and they love her. Her name is Chloe *Gillach*. That is her identity. She was chosen by Tim and Lori, who sacrificed time and money and energy to bring her into their home where she has been shown each and every day that she is sacred, special and dearly loved. As she has grown she has come to understand the sacrifice made by Lori and Tim to make her their child. Adopted children know, perhaps even more than biological children, that they were *chosen*.

You and I have been chosen by God. We were in a dark and hopeless place, lost and alone, when God, through the Spirit, spoke into our hearts and bore witness with our spirit that we are children of God:

> For you did not receive a spirit that makes you a slave
> again to fear, but you received the Spirit of sonship.
> And by him we cry, "*Abba,* Father." The Spirit himself
> testifies with our spirit that we are God's children.
> (Romans 8:15-16 NIV 1984)

Now we live without fear. We are not slaves, we are children. We were chosen by God, who went to the furthest reaches to find us, and sacrificed everything to make us his because in his eyes we are holy and dearly loved.

LIVING INTO THE TRUTH

As mentioned above, we come to know and understand God's love for us by the work of the Holy Spirit. It is the Spirit who bears witness with our spirit that we are children of God, chosen and adopted into the family of God—Father, Son and Spirit. Today, or this week, ask the Holy Spirit to deepen your grasp of the height and depth of God's love for you. Pray specifically that your sacred worth would become clearer to you than before. Then live in such a way that you honor your own value.

AFFIRMATION

God has chosen me—not merely all people—but me specifically, because in his eyes I am holy and in his heart I am dearly loved. I will live this day with the confidence and courage that comes from knowing that I have been *chosen* by him to live forever with him.

PRAYER

Gracious Abba, I give you thanks for all that you have done to bring me into your family of faith. Jesus, you willingly went to the cross that I might be rescued from the dominion of darkness and transferred into the kingdom of light. Thank you for choosing me and making me your child, holy and dearly loved. Amen.

REFLECTION

When you were growing up, did you have a strong sense from your parents or some other relative that you were special and loved? If so, what helped you to feel that way?

20

BELOVED

As God's chosen ones, holy and **beloved** . . .

COLOSSIANS 3:12 (NRSV)

Recently my wife, Meghan, and I were having dinner with our close friends Jennifer and Trevor Hinz and their infant son, Max, who was approaching his tenth month. I watched as Jen fed him from a bottle. Max put his little hands on the bottle and looked into his mother's eyes, eyes that were smiling, eyes full of love for him. Even with the bottle in his mouth, I saw Max begin to smile, and a little milk ran down his cheek. Max didn't care about the messy milk; he was captivated by his mother's love. Jen's love beamed through her eyes and into his, and Max knew he was loved. His smile in return was a beautiful, and holy, moment for me.

That moment brought to mind one of my favorite quotes from theologian Hans Urs von Balthasar. It reads,

> After a mother has smiled at her child for many days and weeks, she finally receives her child's smile in response. She has awakened love in the heart of her child. God interprets himself to man as love in the same way; he radiates love, which kindles the light of love in the heart of man, and it is precisely this light that allows man to perceive this, the absolute Love. Insofar as we are his creatures, the seed of love lies dormant within us as the image of God (*imago*). But just as no child can be awakened to love without being loved, so too no human heart can come to an understanding of God without the free gift of his grace—in the image of his Son.

Notice that phrase in the second sentence: "awakened love." According to Balthasar, little Max has "the seed of love" within him, lying dormant, until a deep love outside of him awakens it. Jennifer's love for Max, radiating in her authentic smile, tells Max, without words, that he is her beloved.

Balthasar uses this experience between a mother and her child as an illustration of how all of us come to know that we are the beloved of God. A seed of love is planted into each of our souls, a deep longing to be loved, but it can only be awakened by being deeply loved. Our deepest longing is to be loved by our Creator. If we knew we were loved, truly loved by God, *as we are*, our souls would be whole. Sadly, very few people know that they are loved. We live in a world of competition, separation, isolation, performance and reward. We are taught from an early age that love must be merited by our behavior, and we project this onto God: "God loves only the good little girls and boys," as the saying goes. It is narrative spun in the pit of hell, and the source of all human suffering.

The cross of Jesus Christ shouts that we are loved—as we are, not as we should be. We are never going to be "as we should be," as if there were some perfect version of us that we must strive to be in order to deserve love and, until then, we must live in shame. Guilt does not produce holiness, only shame, hiding and separation. God, in Jesus, reveals the great mystery: God is love, and we are his beloved. He did not enter into our world to condemn it (John 3:17). He became one of us to reconcile us to God, to remind us that Love itself has created us and calls us home.

In Colossians 3:12, Paul tells us that we are God's chosen ones, holy and beloved. Nowhere does he qualify that with some clause about our behavior: "You are God's beloved . . . if you stop sinning so much." He is telling us a fact about our essential nature. God picked us. He made us holy by infusing his sacred self into us. We are his beloved. This is our truest identity. The world will tell us that we are valued by how we look or by what we accomplish. The Spirit testifies to us that God created us, that we are sacred and that we are "the apple of his eye." If God had a wallet, our picture would be in it. If

God had a refrigerator, our picture would be on it.

The word Paul uses for "beloved" is a perfect participle. This is important. A perfect participle refers to a *completed action* with present and future ramifications. Our being loved is a completed action. The matter is settled. Paul expressed the same sentiment in Galatians 2:20:

> I have been crucified with Christ and I no longer live, but Christ lives in me. The life I now live in the body, I live by faith in the Son of God, who *loved* me and gave himself for me.

Paul lives by faith in Jesus, who loved him and gave himself for him. Let me reverse the order: gave, loved, faith. Jesus *gave* himself. His death for us was the supreme act of love, making undeniable the fact that we are loved. So Paul can say, "I am *loved*." But how does he know it? He knows it by *faith*. Faith is the fundamental response to the love offered up to us.

We come to know that we are loved by the ministry of the Holy Spirit, whose main work is to point us to the love of God, as seen most vividly in the cross. The Spirit is God's smile shining on us, urging us to know that we are loved. As stated, it has nothing to do with our merit. Again, von Balthasar explains, "God has already seen in him, the loveless sinner, a beloved child and has looked upon him and conferred dignity upon him in the light of this love." Just as Jennifer loves Max before he can love her back, so God loves us "loveless sinners," and in so doing confers dignity upon us. We are God's beloved. God does not love us because we have earned it; it is his gift to us.

And it is a gift that transforms. Too many of us believe the lie that if we just try harder to be good, to love more, to serve better, then God will be pleased with us. This never produced anything but guilt and shame, isolating us from God and from one another. The truth that we are unconditionally loved leads us to the only place where we can truly love. The radiant smile of God penetrates our soul and awakens us to our holiness, strengthening us and leading us to love and serve. Our lives are called to be a response to God's self-giving love. Every good thing we do in this life—love, forgive, serve—is merely an echo of the love of God.

God is smiling at you.

Can you see it?

LIVING INTO THE TRUTH

This week ask the Spirit to reveal to you that you are God's beloved. This is a deep and important prayer. Sit quietly and ask the Spirit over and over, "Show me God's love for me, blessed Holy Spirit." Remain quiet and wait. Listen with the ears of your heart.

AFFIRMATION

I am God's chosen, holy and beloved child.

PRAYER

Gracious Abba, thank you for sending your Spirit to show me
that I am loved. In a world that tells me love must be earned,
strengthen my faith; help me to believe that I am loved as I
am. Let me live and believe that I am loved. Amen.

REFLECTION

Why is this fundamental truth (that we are God's beloved) so
difficult for so many of us to believe?

21

BEAR

Bear *with each other . . .*

COLOSSIANS 3:13

*D*uring my first pastorate in the local church I assembled a "spiritual formation" group. I invited everyone from the pulpit, and seven people signed up. We met together for over two years.

We were a very heterogeneous group in terms of age, gender and life situation. Our diversity made it more difficult to connect with each other at first, but in time that diversity provided for rich interaction. Our gatherings were a great blessing and benefit to me. At the same time we all brought our faults and foibles with us each week.

One member was a young man in his twenties who was

very conservative theologically and very rigid. Anytime someone said something other than what he believed, he started a debate, and the person he disagreed with would often feel hurt, or fight back. He was actually a sweet person and had a servant's heart, but this one area of his character was difficult to bear, and it showed up each week.

A grandmother in the group was a recent widow, and her deep sadness over the death of her husband came through the door with her each week. Every few weeks she would begin sobbing as she shared about her life. Though no one blamed her, we all felt her sorrow as it darkened the room.

There was a middle-aged mother of teenagers whose struggles with her children would often dominate the discussion. I was not a parent yet, and I found myself internally judging the way she parented them. Her sharing became a way to vent her frustration, which we all accepted, but after hearing the same things over and over, we began to wear down. Once, when she was absent, one of the members openly criticized her parenting skills, and soon others began to agree. I gently tried to end the judge-fest.

Also in the group was a young woman who was very shy and seldom spoke. When she did it was usually profound and insightful. I would tell her, outside of the group, that she should speak more because she had so much to offer. When one of her parents became ill, she was terribly distraught about it and became even more distant.

I was only twenty-six at the time, fresh out of seminary

and not very self-aware. Looking back, I am certain that my flaws and issues were a drain on them. My biggest flaw, I see now, was trying to be more spiritual and wise than I actually was. As a result, I was seldom really honest with them, fearing that if I seemed weak or uncertain or did not have an answer, they would look down on me. So I ended up putting on a mask, and they had to endure that. I never let them get to know the real me—my hurts and fears and struggles. I only let them see the mask.

The truth about all community—secular or sacred—is that it consists of people, and people are flawed. Paul encouraged the Colossian Christians to "*bear* with each other" (3:13). The virtues he listed in 3:12 (compassion, kindness, gentleness, humility and patience) must express themselves in the act of forbearing. This is what we did every week in our group. Each one of us brought in our flaws and struggles and weaknesses, giving the others the opportunity to bear with each other.

I used to think of this as a burden and often wished that everyone on the group would become what I wanted them to be. I wanted the rigid young man to be less rigid and more accepting. I wanted the widow to get over her loss. I wanted the mother of the teenagers to quit whining and be a better parent. I wanted the shy young woman to be more outgoing. And I wanted to be more transparent with them but failed to take the risk.

My friend Rich Mullins wrote a song called "Brother's Keeper." In it he sings, "My friends ain't the way I wish they were, they are just the way they are." None of us has it all together, and if we are going to live in community we will have to learn to accept others as they are, not as we want them to be.

That does not mean that we simply accept the flaws and stop wanting people to change. The rigid young man would have benefitted from being less judgmental, as would all of us. What it does mean is that we welcome the opportunity to bear the burdens of others. But more than that, I have come to believe that it is a privilege to bear the burdens of others. When we bear with one another we experience genuine love and intimacy. It is an opportunity, not an obligation.

Bearing with one another is the only way to love and be loved. To this day I cannot recall a single conversation we had in that group. But what I do remember is how we loved one another, imperfectly, to be sure. The young man's rigidity, the widow's sorrow and the mother's whining allowed us to exercise compassion, kindness, gentleness, humility and patience.

In Galatians 6:2 Paul wrote, "Bear one another's burdens, and in this way you will fulfill the law of Christ" (NRSV). The way of Jesus is to bear the burdens of others. This is exactly what Jesus has done for each of us, and in so doing he has given us an example and a motive for bearing with each other.

A few years ago I was speaking at a Christian high school, and several members of that formation group came to support me. After it was over we all found a place to sit down and reminisce. The young man who was so unyielding in his doctrine (now a middle-aged man) asked to have coffee someday, and we did, a few weeks later. He said, "So much has happened in my life over the past twenty years, and it has really changed me. I used to be so dogmatic and argumentative, but now I'm not that way as much. I'm still pretty conservative in what I believe. I just don't need to pick a fight. How did you all put up with me in our small group?" I told him that we all had issues, but those flaws gave us an opportunity to truly love one another. He agreed.

The great challenge in community comes from the reality that none of us has it all together. As a consequence, our faults and flaws become a burden for those around us.

LIVING INTO THE TRUTH

Today, or this week, engage in the Jesus way by bearing with the people you live and work with. Pick one person whose faults or flaws or problems have been a burden for you to bear. Begin by praying for them. Instead of thinking of their struggles as an obligation, see them as an opportunity to demonstrate love—in the form of compassion, kindness, gentleness, humility and patience.

AFFIRMATION

The struggles, problems and weaknesses of those around me are not an obligation for me, but an opportunity for me to demonstrate the love of Jesus.

PRAYER

Gracious Abba, just as you have borne all of my burdens with gladness, help me to demonstrate that love to the people I live and work with. Give me your eyes of compassion, and teach me how to see their struggles as an opportunity to demonstrate real love. Amen.

REFLECTION

When have you been in a situation where it was difficult to get along because of the personal issues or struggles of those in the community?

FORGIVE

Bear with each other and **forgive** *one another*
if any of you has a grievance against someone.
Forgive *as the Lord forgave you.*

COLOSSIANS 3:13

In addition to teaching us to bear one another's burdens, living in community makes it necessary to learn the art of forgiveness. People harm each other—that is a reality of human existence. Sometimes it is slight, such as not showing us the respect we deserve. Perhaps we are overlooked or uninvited. Sometimes it is a deeper hurt, such as unfaithfulness or intentional malice. Each of us has been harmed by others in some way, because all of us are flawed and broken and sinful.

Jesus, our master teacher, once said, "And when you stand praying, if you hold anything against anyone, forgive them, so that your Father in heaven may forgive you your sins" (Mark 11:25). He gave several illustrations, through parables, about the necessity of forgiving others because we ourselves have been forgiven (see Matthew 18:21-35). We can easily make the mistake of thinking that divine forgiveness is determined by human forgiveness—in other words, to think that God only forgives me if I forgive others, and in the exact measure that I forgive others. Clearly this is not the way of the new covenant, where Jesus' act of divine forgiveness was once and for all, and not dependent on anything we do (Romans 5:8).

So what is Jesus telling us when he instructs us to forgive others? And why does he connect it with the forgiveness of God? He wants us to know that if we desire forgiveness, we must enter into the sphere of God's mercy. And if we enter into that sphere of mercy, we cannot receive forgiveness without being willing to offer it to others. There are few one-way streets in the kingdom.

We cannot say, "I accept God's forgiveness for my sins, but I refuse to forgive others." This is actually impossible, not just theologically but psychologically. If we truly know—in the depths of our being—that we have been completely forgiven, then we will naturally forgive those who have harmed us in some way. It may take time—it often does—and it may involve the help of another, particularly a good counselor or therapist who listens, understands and can guide us.

When we do find ourselves struggling to forgive someone, we should not grit our teeth and merely try harder to forgive them. Instead, we should dwell on the fundamental reality that we ourselves are people who need forgiveness, and then set our minds on the reality that God, in Christ, has forgiven us completely.

When I plumb the depths of my own heart, I see an unwillingness to forgive others. Recently I experienced disappointment at being overlooked by someone. For several weeks I carried the pain and disappointment in my heart in the form of unforgiveness and a cool anger toward the person who overlooked me. But our hearts cannot live with the hypocrisy of making the two-way street a one-way street. The Spirit gently spoke to me over the course of a few months. In that time I discovered that the real problem I had in this matter had nothing to do with the person who overlooked me. It had to do with me and, in particular, my *pride*.

The reason we are hard on others, and even hard on ourselves, is because we are proud. I realized that I did not want to admit I am a creature who lives each day by mercy. I like to think that I am special and powerful and deserving of the good things that happen to me. In reality, I am utterly unworthy of everything good in my life. I was *given* life, great parents, a healthy body, air to breathe, food to eat, friends and family to love me, and endless opportunities—all completely undeserved. And in truth, I have sinned countless times and have been *given* forgiveness—completely unearned.

As Christians, mercy and grace are the atmosphere we live in. But there is something in us that resists accepting them. Instead we try to earn them through performance and physical prowess. We easily accept the false narrative that tells us we are strong and powerful and can do anything and be anything, by our own efforts—and that when we do the world will be impressed. It is much harder to accept the narrative that we are all highly dependent, extremely unworthy beneficiaries of unending grace. So when we are harmed by someone, we feel the affront. Our pride is wounded, and we are poised to fight back. One way we fight back is to refuse to forgive. But when we do so, we deny reality.

We forgive when we know, truly know, we have been, and will be, forgiven by a merciful God. We forgive others when we look at Jesus, our master and model, who willingly humbled himself, took the form of a servant, and gave his very life as a visible demonstration of forgiveness and reconciliation. Paul tells the Colossians, "*Forgive* as the Lord forgave you" (3:13). And we not only forgive *as* the Lord forgave us, not merely *because* the Lord forgave us; we forgive *with* the Lord. We can only forgive when we know and feel the presence of Jesus standing with us, the One who is the model but also the *means* of forgiveness. That's why the first thing I do when I am harmed is to pray for the grace to forgive.

In truth, we receive forgiveness in far greater measure than we will ever have to emulate. Jesus has forgiven me thousands of sins, much more than I will need to forgive in my lifetime. As the Spirit began to teach me about my unwillingness to forgive the person who overlooked me, he showed me my deep need for mercy and pity, as well as the need to have mercy and pity on the person who—in my estimation—harmed me.

I came to see that the barrier to forgiveness was my own pride, which simply makes life miserable. So I prayed and prayed, and after a few months I was able to forgive. This did not right the "wrong" done to me. After all, forgiveness is not about justice; it is about healing. A feeling of freedom and release came over me. I felt the Spirit smiling with me inside. I knew what James meant when he wrote, "Mercy triumphs over judgment" (James 2:13)!

LIVING INTO THE TRUTH

Are you carrying a spirit of unforgiveness toward someone? If so, begin by praying for the grace to forgive. Ask the Spirit to search your heart, to reveal any barrier that might be preventing you from forgiving that person. Do not expect this to happen overnight. It may take time to begin to understand why it's difficult to forgive that individual. You cannot expect the person to change or to ask for forgiveness. This is a matter of your own heart. Do expect God to be with you in this process.

AFFIRMATION

God has forgiven me. I live in an atmosphere of grace. Therefore, I can—by his grace—forgive those who harm me. Forgiveness is not about justice; it is about healing.

PRAYER

Gracious Abba, thank you for forgiving me for all of my sins. I have sinned against you far more than others have sinned against me. You are my model, and you are my means for forgiving others. By your grace, help me to forgive as you have forgiven me. Amen.

REFLECTION

Have you been hurt by someone, and found it difficult to forgive them? Explain.

23

LOVE

*And over all these virtues put on **love**,*
which binds them all together in perfect unity.

Colossians 3:14

*E*ach time we fly on an airplane we hear the mandatory flight-safety instructions. We hear about exit lights and float cushions under our seat. And we hear the counterintuitive advice about the oxygen mask that will drop down in case of an emergency landing: "In the unlikely event of an emergency landing, an oxygen mask will drop down. If you are traveling with a small child, be sure to secure your mask first before assisting them." I call this counterintuitive because, as a parent, my first reaction would be to make sure my child had his or her mask on first. But this could be bad if you failed to get oxygen yourself and lost consciousness; then both you and your child could be in danger. The instruction is clear: take care of yourself first; if you don't, you put others at risk.

Every time I hear those instructions I think about the Great Commandment. Jesus was once asked what the greatest commandment was, and he responded, "The most important one . . . is this: 'Hear, O Israel: the Lord our God, the Lord is one. Love the Lord your God with all your heart and with all your soul and with all your mind and with all your strength.' The second is this: 'Love your neighbor as yourself.' There is no commandment greater than these" (Mark 12:29-31).

Jesus' response has a clear order: first, love God; second, love your neighbor. The order is important because the love we extend to our neighbor is the same love we receive from God. If we are not in a deep, intimate, loving relationship with God, we will not be able to extend genuine Christian (*agapé*) love to others. Just as parents need to have their own oxygen mask secure and working before helping their child, so we must first breathe the pure air of the kingdom of God before we can lead others into it. We can only love others genuinely when we make it our primary aim to integrate our little kingdoms and queendoms with the kingdom of God, for it is there that we experience authentic, unconditional and eternal love. That's why Jesus tells us elsewhere, "Seek first his kingdom and his righteousness, and all these things will be given to you as well" (Matthew 6:33).

When we enroll as apprentices of Jesus and place our trust in him, we engage in a relationship of deep and abiding love. As we do so, we become strong. We all need, more than anything else, to know that we are loved, to know that we are cared for, to be certain that we are safe and valued. We long to be accepted as we are. The world we live in cannot offer this. No human being can offer this. There is only one place we can find this love we so desperately need: in the Trinity. The gospel meta-narrative is a story about love— God's love for each of us and his willingness to suffer and die to draw us into this life of love. Our modern culture is in love with the idea of love, but it does not know how to love without condition. In our world the narrative is clear: we find love and acceptance and worth only through performance, by earning it. Love can be won, and love can be lost. It is not really love at all.

Love is not dependent on our actions but is a condition of being. We learn to reside habitually in the kingdom of God's love. And in that sphere of existence we feel God's smile and hear God singing over us, and our hearts are "strangely warmed." We no longer need the world's approval to feel valid. We learn to let go of pride and the need to succeed. We are loved. And we respond to the embrace of God's love by loving God in return, with our heart, soul, mind and strength. Then, and only then, can we truly love others. The kingdom of God has a clear order.

In one of the most famous passages in the Bible, Paul writes,

Love is patient, love is kind. It does not envy, it does not boast, it is not proud. It does not dishonor others, it is not self-seeking, it is not easily angered, it keeps no record of wrongs. Love does not delight in evil but rejoices with the truth. It always protects, always trusts, always hopes, always perseveres. Love never fails. (1 Corinthians 13:4-8)

Though we most often hear these verses at weddings, as if they were describing the love between a man and a woman, they are actually talking about the love of God, a love that is patient and kind, keeps no record of wrongs, and never fails. Paul then tells the Corinthians, "Pursue love" (1 Corinthians 14:1 NRSV). The image here is of hunting down and catching love. When we catch—or rather, are caught by—love, we become lovers of others.

God's love is patient and kind, never jealous or proud or self-seeking. God's love protects and trusts and hopes. And when we catch that love, we begin to love in the same way. In Colossians 3:14 Paul offers the capstone to the entire chapter so far. We who have set our minds on things above, whose life is secure and hidden with Jesus, who have put our old, sinful self to death, who live in unity with people who are different from us, who have clothed ourselves with compassion, kindness, humility, gentleness and patience, are now to put on the final garment: love.

Love is the final piece of clothing that makes it all work together. God dresses us in his unfailing, eternal love. Now we can love as God loves. My neighbors don't merit my love by anything they do. My love for my neighbors is a response to the reality that they are a gift of God. If Jesus has died for my neighbors and taken away their guilt (as he has mine), then I must learn to see them as they look in the eyes of my Father. The world's word about my neighbors—that they must earn the right to be loved—is false. God's word about my neighbors is true: they are sacred treasures.

The invisible trinitarian community of love becomes visible in our love for one another. This is the reciprocity of love found in the economy of God's kingdom. John said it best: "we love because [God] first loved us" (1 John 4:19).

LIVING INTO THE TRUTH

The order of the kingdom is clear: we are first loved by God, then we extend that love to others. Today, or this week, saturate your mind with the reality of God's love. One of the best ways to do this is to focus on the incarnation, the willingness of Jesus to become human in order to save us—the greatest act of love. I have found that by reading, and slowly rereading, Philippians 2:5-11, I begin to discover the richness of God's love in Christ. These verses might have been an early Christian hymn, or perhaps a poem penned by Paul. Either way, they are a beautiful depiction of God's love for us. As you set your mind on these words, ask the Spirit to deepen your awareness and confidence in God's love for you. Then ask the Spirit to bring people into your midst that you can begin extending this love to.

AFFIRMATION

God's love for me never fails. As I learn to dwell in this love I will naturally begin to love others in the same way that God loves me: with patience, kindness, and keeping no record of wrongs. I can love, because God first loved me.

PRAYER

Gracious Abba, your love is the greatest gift of my life. Help me to know it not just in my head but in my heart. May your love become such a deep reality that my heart begins to swell with joy and hope. And may I offer that same kind of love to those I live and work with, and everyone I meet this day. Amen.

REFLECTION

What would your life look like if you genuinely, fully and perfectly understood God's love for you?

24

PEACE

*Let the **peace** of Christ rule in your hearts,*
since as members of one body you were called to peace.

COLOSSIANS 3:15

Over the past twenty-five years I have had the privilege of serving on several ministry boards and committees. In that span of time, two boards—and two very different meetings—stand out to me. Both boards were made up of men and women who were committed Christians, people who honestly strove to follow the Spirit and further the work of the kingdom of God. Yet each of these boards went about their business in very different ways, with very different results. For the sake of distinction, I will call one Board A and the other Board B.

Board A had several passionate, opinionated and out-spoken members. Because I am, by nature, more even-keeled (so they said) and am decent at resolving conflict, they chose me to be the chair of the board. I had never been a board chair, so I declined, but they were persistent and eventually I accepted. Each of the meetings that followed became tumultuous. People came with very clear, conflicting ideas, which led to debates, and ultimately to arguments and accusations. It wasn't uncommon for someone to storm out of the room during a meeting. Over time I lost control of the board, and within a few years the organization disbanded.

Board B also had several passionate, opinionated and out-spoken members. Fortunately I was not saddled with being the chair of that board, but, in hindsight, I might have been able to handle it, for one reason: the members of Board B were women and men whose hearts beat first and foremost for Jesus and his kingdom. They tackled challenging issues and at times disagreed, but the disagreements never degenerated into debates. They would politely discuss the issue and isolate any disagreement, and then decide to consider the matter prayerfully. I will never forget one meeting in particular, in which we could not resolve an issue. One of the members said, "Let's table this until tomorrow, and let's each spend some time in prayer tonight and tomorrow before we reconvene." We did, and the meeting the next morning was peaceful and productive.

I do not want to appear to be judging Board A and portraying them as lesser apprentices of Jesus. Board A did some fine work over the years, and when the time came to make changes, they did. When they disbanded, they parted as friends, and God has blessed each members' further efforts. The difference between Board A and Board B is how they worked together in community. As we have seen in the last few chapters, living and working with others will naturally require us to bear each other's burdens, forgive one another and love each other. It also requires that we learn how to disagree and work through our problems.

The key to this is peace. In our present verse Paul writes, "Let the *peace* of Christ rule in your hearts, since as members of one body you were called to peace" (Colossians 3:15). Peace is not merely the absence of strife; it is the presence of harmony. And peace is not merely a concept, such as not harming someone. The songwriter John Lennon famously wrote, "all we are saying is give peace a chance." This has always failed because the notion of peace itself is simply an idea. Notice what Paul wrote: "let the peace *of Christ* rule . . ." The idea of peace is not what solves conflict; it is the peace of Jesus that provides the power we need to live and work in harmony.

Jesus said, "Peace I leave with you; *my peace* I give you. I do not give to you as the world gives" (John 14:27). The world cannot give this kind of peace. It cannot even comprehend this peace. The peace of Jesus "surpasses all understanding" (Philippians 4:7 NRSV). What is the peace of Jesus?

It is "the peace which belongs to His kingdom by virtue of his sovereignty." Jesus rules and reigns over all: all creation, all humanity and all history. When we step into his reign (the kingdom of God), we step into his peace. We can now live in constant interaction with Jesus, and because of his protection, guidance and provision, we have nothing to fear and can live with sheer confidence.

In verse 15 Paul uses a word found only once in the entire New Testament, the Greek word *brabeueto*, translated "rule": let the peace of Christ *rule* in your hearts . . ." The word was sometimes used for an umpire or referee in sporting events. It was also used for someone who served as an arbitrator. J. B. Lightfoot says of this verse, "Where there is a conflict of motives or desires, the peace of Christ must step in and decide which is to prevail." That is precisely what Board B was able to do that Board A was not. Board B consisted of members who knew how to let the peace of Christ be the deciding factor when they ran into disagreement.

Letting the peace of Christ rule in our hearts is the same as setting our minds on things above (Colossians 3:2). Paul also refers to this as letting our minds be controlled by the Spirit: "the mind controlled by the Spirit is life and *peace*" (Romans 8:6 NIV 1984). The members of Board B knew how to set their minds on the things of the Spirit, how to look at issues with the greater principles of the kingdom of God in mind. In the kingdom of God we are safe, secure, valued and assured that God is with us.

Strife is often the result of people being disconnected from the kingdom, not united to Jesus, and in that place of weakness they latch on to their position or argument as if their value depended on it. This is why so many churches split apart. At some point the focus is taken off of Jesus and his kingdom and another issue is allowed to become more important. When that happens, Jesus is no longer the focus; the area of disagreement is. As a result, the "one body" to which we were called becomes fractured and breaks apart.

For the peace of Christ to rule in a community, it must first rule in the hearts of the individuals who compose it. That will only happen when we immerse ourselves in the reality and glory of God's rule and reign. Then, and only then, will we receive the peace of Christ, a peace that the world cannot give, a peace that surpasses all understanding.

LIVING INTO THE TRUTH

We bear each other's burdens as Christ has borne ours. We forgive one another as Christ has forgiven us. We love because God first loved us. In the same way, peace is not something we manufacture; it is a gift bestowed on us by Jesus. Today, or this week, live in close connection with Jesus. Make it your effort to live in constant interaction with Jesus, receiving his protection, provision and guidance. As you do, pay attention to how you interact with others. You may notice that you are bringing the peace of Christ into each relationship and interaction.

AFFIRMATION

Jesus offers me his peace, the peace found in living under the rule and reign of God. When this rules in my heart, I live in peace, with myself and with everyone I interact with.

PRAYER

Gracious Abba, I so badly need your peace. I need it in my own heart, and I need it in the many relationships I have. Help me to see and feel your presence and power, your protection and provision, and to live in peace and harmony with everyone, even when we disagree. Amen.

REFLECTION

How can you let the peace of Christ rule in your heart today?

25

THANKFUL

And be **thankful**.

Colossians 3:15

I was recently in England speaking to a group of about thirty men and women who are active in ministry in some way. After a brief talk, I broke them down into small groups with one discussion question: "What is a recent spiritual practice that has been a blessing in your life?"

My group consisted of a man and two women in addition to myself. One of the women said, "I'll go first. About a year ago I started something I am calling a 'Gratitude Journal.' Each day, at the end of the day, I write down five things that happened that day that were either fun or delicious or entertaining or uplifting."

I asked, "Do you do it every night?" She said, "Most of the time. I rarely forget to do it. I have it by my bed, and it is the last thing I do each night."

"What has been the benefit in your spiritual life?" I asked.

"Well," she said, "I found myself neglecting to really pay attention to all of the good things in my life. That's why I started doing it. But as I began doing it, I began to develop a more thankful heart. Each day I see the goodness of life more and more, and I appreciate it more than I used to. I often took things for granted, as if I deserved them. And when things did not go as I wanted them to, I would whine about it. Now I see that everything is a gift to be savored, and I express my gratitude to God each day for all of the wonderful things he brings my way."

I was both convicted and encouraged by her example. That is one of the great things about Christian community— we inspire each other simply through our own experiences and testimony. That evening I attended a concert at St. Martin's in the Field, and in their gift shop I noticed a beautiful little journal. The Spirit nudged me, reminding me of what she had shared, and I immediately took it to the counter and bought it. Later that night I began the very same practice she had been doing, writing down five things that had happened that day that were a blessing to me. My opening entry in my gratitude journal was the testimony of this young woman that the Spirit used to inspire me.

In this section of Colossians 3 (vv. 15-17), Paul urges his

readers to be thankful three times: in verse 15, "And be thankful"; in verse 16, "with gratitude"; and in verse 17, "giving thanks." I didn't see the connection when I first memorized the passage, but now I see it clearly. This begs the question: Why is being thankful so important to Paul? What is it about gratitude that is so essential in our lives? How does being thankful enhance our spiritual lives? As I began answering these questions, I ran into some false narratives about thankfulness that, unfortunately, many Christians believe.

One false notion many Christians have is that gratitude is required—even demanded—by God, and that our ingratitude will be punished. When I see someone receive something as a gift and not be grateful, it bothers me. After someone gives their child something, parents often say to the child, "What do you say?" and the child then remembers to say, "Thank you." I think we transfer this experience onto God and assume that God is looking at us and our ingratitude, wanting to scream out, "What do you say?"

In truth, God wants nothing for himself. God is not like us. He is complete in himself. And as One who loves genuinely, he demands nothing in return. He freely gives to us without any strings. And yet, the only proper response to the myriad gifts he gives to us is gratitude and thanksgiving.

The other false view I have heard is that thanksgiving is the secret ingredient needed for getting our prayers answered. After all, Paul said, "Do not be anxious about anything, but in everything, by prayer and petition, *with thanksgiving*, present your requests to God" (Philippians 4:6 NIV 1984). But if we make offering thanks to God a way to get what we want, then we are distorting Paul's real message—that we can be thankful for a God who listens.

When Paul urges the Colossians to be thankful three times, each is for a different reason. The first thing we ought to be thankful for is that God has *chosen* us: "as members of one body you were called to peace. And be thankful" (3:15). You were chosen by God, selected to be a member of the body of Jesus. How amazing is that? God chose you! You are now a member of God's family, rescued and adopted.

Second, we are to be thankful for how the word of Christ dwells in us, transforming our hearts with the truth of the gospel and thus leading us to sing "with gratitude in [our] hearts to God" (3:16). The gospel—which is never ending and always new—is a gift we should always be grateful for.

The third gift we are to be thankful for is, well, everything! Paul writes, "Whatever you do . . . do it all . . . giving thanks to God" (3:17). We live in the strong and unshakable kingdom of God, where resources are plentiful. Every moment of every day is a gift, full of wonder, if only we have the eyes to see it. We have been called and chosen to enter into fellowship with God and his people. We have been given the word of Christ, the gospel, that has been bearing fruit throughout the world for over two thousand years. We have been given air and food and shelter and family and friends and sunsets and starlight and ice cream and music—and all things.

All of it is a gift. And when we see all of life that way, we conclude as the young woman who kept a gratitude journal did: "Now I see that everything is a gift to be savored, and I express my gratitude to God each day for all of the wonderful things he brings my way."

A gift to be savored. A gift to be thankful for. That is what our lives are.

LIVING INTO THE TRUTH

Today, or this week, begin keeping a gratitude journal. Try to write down five things that happened to you each day that were a blessing to you. Do not feel the need to make everything "spiritual"; if you enjoyed a delicious slice of pizza or a funny movie, simply write it down. The cumulative effect of these small moments of pleasure will, over time, amount to a large amount of gratitude and thanksgiving.

AFFIRMATION

All of life is a gift—undeserved but given by a loving God who does not demand my thanks, but for whom thanks and praise are the only right and good responses.

PRAYER

Gracious Abba, thank you for choosing me, and bringing me into your family. Thank you for the gospel, the good news that has transformed my life. And thank you for everything good and perfect in my life. All of it is a gift that comes from you. May I live with a constant attitude of gratitude each day. Amen.

REFLECTION

How would you rate yourself in terms of your ability to see everything as a gift from God?

26

WORD

Let the **word** *of Christ dwell in you richly.*

COLOSSIANS 3:16 (NRSV)

*E*arly in my Christian life I learned that the more I spent time reading, studying and memorizing the Bible, the more my life reflected the character of Christ. In one of my earliest journal entries, at the age of nineteen, I wrote, "The Word keeps me from sin; and sin keeps me from the Word." The Bible, the living Word of God, was an essential part of my daily life with God.

At college I joined a Christian fellowship that met every Wednesday evening. It was led by a few upperclassmen whose faith was more grounded than mine. Each week one of them would give a talk based on a passage of the Bible. I found their teachings to be inspiring. I marked up my Bible as they went along, making notes in the margins. I was also in a weekly Bible study with two other guys. We spent most of the semester studying the letter to the Romans. Week by week my knowledge of God grew, as did my faith.

Eventually I transferred to a Christian college and then went on to seminary. This allowed me to take dozens of classes in theology, Bible and church history. I even took Greek and Hebrew. I felt I knew the Bible, that I could handle doing exegesis (the science of interpreting a text), and thus could preach and teach accurately. I thought I knew the Bible as well as anyone. In truth, looking back, I became a bit of a snob.

Then something unexpected happened.

My faith life began to die. I found myself unable to pray and, at times, not even wanting to pray. The inner emptiness was shocking to me because I had developed a vibrant relationship with God that had driven and sustained me. I was blessed to sit under the teaching of Richard Foster as an undergraduate, who taught me the art of Bible contemplation, sometimes called *lectio divina*, where you sit before a passage of the Bible and let it speak to you. But it was no longer speaking. Or if it was, I was no longer able to listen.

I shared my struggle with a fellow seminarian, and he encouraged me to go with him on a five-day silent retreat at an Episcopal monastery. That sounded daunting to me, but I was desperate. So I agreed.

Part of the retreat included an hour a day with a spiritual

director, a ministry the monks at the monastery provided for free. The first day I met with my director and told him of my emptiness. He gave me a passage of Scripture, Luke 1:26-38, to meditate on. It is the story of the annunciation, where Mary is told by Gabriel that she is to bear the Messiah. "Tomorrow we will meet to discuss what God is speaking to you," my director said.

I went back to my room and began reading and rereading the passage. It was as dry as dust. I had been trained to study, analyze and dissect the Bible. The problem with dissection is that you end up with a dead subject. I went back the next day and shared some scholarly thoughts with the monk, but he was not impressed. "Go back and sit before this passage again, and we will talk tomorrow."

I was disappointed. I found the passage to be just "a boring birth narrative." Again, nothing happened, and I felt terribly alone. The next day I shared my lack of insight, and he said, "Jim, how do you fall asleep?"

I said, "I lie in bed and turn out the lights."

"Right," he said, "you create the conditions for sleep. You cannot make yourself fall asleep, but you can create the conditions for it. It is the same with contemplation of the Bible. You can't force God to speak, and in the same sense, God won't force his word on you. You have to create the conditions by sitting still, by being willing to hear, and through surrender. When you surrender yourself to the passage, the Spirit will speak."

That afternoon I tried and tried, and failed and failed.

Then, sometime after dinner, I went back again, this time utterly broken. I prayed, "God, please speak to me. I am ready to hear whatever you have for me."

I read the passage one more time. Almost immediately the words seemed different, alive and new. I found myself standing in Mary's place, hearing the angel's word to me as if I were her. "Be not afraid," the angel said to her (and to me), and the Spirit began speaking to me about my fears. A gentle comfort came over me. I knew that God was with me.

It was one of the richest two hours of my life. I felt God's presence and heard God's voice. At the very end I was finally able to say with Mary, "Let it be unto me."

In verse 16 Paul tells the Colossians, "Let the word of Christ dwell in you richly." The word of Christ is the teaching of Jesus, transmitted to us by the written word and interpreted by the Holy Spirit. Paul uses the word "dwell" to describe our relationship to the word of Christ. It literally means "live in you," with reference to the inside of a house.

We let the word of Christ live in us when we read, study, memorize and reflect on the Bible—alone or with a small group or a church. Scripture is God's Word that bears witness to Jesus, the Word of God. God longs to communicate with us, to bless and encourage and at times exhort us. The Spirit knows exactly what each of us needs, every single day.

Our part is simply to come to the Word in an attitude of surrender and openness. I had trained myself to be an inter-preter of the Bible, but in truth, the Spirit is the only inter-preter of the Bible. Being able to read scholarly commentaries and know Greek and Hebrew are good and helpful skills. But those skills are not necessary for hearing God and can, in fact, at times get in the way, as they did for me. We let the word of Christ dwell in us richly when we come with a hungry heart, with open ears and with a desire not only to hear but also to do what God calls us to do.

LIVING INTO THE TRUTH

Today, or this week, spend time contemplating Luke 1:26-38. Try to enter into the passage not as a passive viewer but as an active participant. You may even want to try to put yourself in the place of Mary. Try to see and smell and feel and hear what she does. Come with an open heart, ready to hear what the Spirit has uniquely for you. Keep a notebook or journal handy as you may want to write down something God speaks to you.

AFFIRMATION

The word of Christ is a gift from God to me, but can only be received when I come to the Bible with an open and hungry heart to hear what God has for me.

PRAYER

Gracious Abba, thank you for the gift of the Scriptures. They are the primary way you communicate with us. Help me to come before the Bible as one who wants only to hear from you. Give me the word you want me to hear, and may I then ponder it and let it dwell richly within me. Amen.

REFLECTION

Describe a time when God spoke a word directly to you. If you have not had this kind of experience, what are some ways that God communicates with you?

27

TEACH

Teach *and admonish*
one another with all wisdom.

COLOSSIANS 3:16

When we think about great teachers, we often think about pastors and professors. But in truth, most of our teachers are not professionals. They are ordinary men and women who have a genuine relationship with God, through Christ, and God uses them to reach and to teach his people. I have been blessed with great teachers who were professors or preachers. But two primary teachers in my life had no degrees or titles to their name, other than "faithful followers of Jesus."

A year after my experience at the monastery, I returned to seminary for a final year of preparation before graduation. In my final class that year, in the final lecture, my New Testament professor said something I have never forgotten, and something that was very prophetic:

> You are about to graduate from a prestigious school, with a degree that likely no one in your congregation will have. You will be tempted to think that you are the best educated, smartest and wisest person in your community, and to think that you know more about the Bible than all of the people in the church combined. But know this: in each of your churches there will be an older man or an older woman who has no training in biblical studies but who nonetheless knows more about the Bible than you will ever know.

There was a stunned silence in the room. I sensed I had just heard something worth remembering.

Right after I graduated from seminary I was ordained and appointed to a small church in Kansas. In this church I met a man and his wife who would become two of the most important teachers in my life. They had no formal education. He was a simple Kansas farmer, semi-retired by that time and living with his wife of many years. But Leonard and Katherine Deets became my mentors. They would invite me over to their home for lunches during the week and always made time for us to have a cup of coffee and chat.

Leonard and Katherine were deeply committed to Jesus, and had been for their entire lives. The word of Christ dwelled in them richly, and the peace of Christ ruled in their hearts. Though I was the one ordained and appointed to be their spiritual leader, in truth, they were mine. With each passing month I found myself relying more and more on their wisdom. Life as a pastor is filled with difficult situations, trying relationships, and daily challenges. I would try as best I could with my own insight and intuition but would routinely make blunders and missteps. Each time, Leonard would be there to help me get back up, learn from my mistakes and try to be a better pastor. Both he and Katherine attended a Sunday school class I taught and took notes on each session. They were not shy in telling me when I got it right and when I went off track.

Paul encourages the Colossians to "*teach* and admonish one another with all wisdom" (Colossians 3:16). Notice that he does not define a hierarchy of teachers or say, "Those of you ordained should teach . . ." Paul does not assume that he and Epaphras (Paul's colleague who founded the church in Colosse) are the only ones qualified to teach. Instead, it's clear from this text (and Romans 15:14) that Paul expected all Christians to "teach and admonish one another" with wisdom. Every person in the pew bears the privilege and responsibility of teaching. Leonard and Katherine taught me that week after week.

There is a clear logic to this section of Colossians, beginning in 3:10. People are to put on Christ, like a new set of clothes, exhibiting unity, compassion, kindness, humility, gentleness, patience and love. As they do that, the peace of Christ rules over their hearts, hearts in which the word of Christ dwells richly. Such people—like Leonard and Katherine—can and must teach and admonish others. Admonishment, a mild form of correction, is a way of demonstrating the love of Christ. Leonard and Katherine modeled this for me beautifully. They were unassuming, always gentle, never caustic but always unafraid to correct me when I made a mistake. They were God's gift to me, and I thank God that they fulfilled their call of teaching and admonishing me.

Katherine and Leonard Deets also guided me with their wisdom. Within a year of my appointment, our congregation went through a painful period, as one of our leaders was asked by our elders to resign. The church was hurting, and I was asked to assume a larger leadership role than I was prepared to handle. Each day Leonard came to my office and prayed with me. He left me notes of encouragement and helped me navigate what was the most challenging period of my professional life. When things got especially difficult, Leonard would look at me and smile. "Jesus is Lord, Jim. We don't need to worry about anything." Then he would throw his head back and laugh and pat me on the back. "We'll be okay. God is with us." It was very healing.

A few years after I left that church, Katherine died. Leonard lived alone for many years, and then his children moved him closer to them, in the Northwest, into a retirement community. Each year, Leonard sends my wife and me a card on our anniversary. It is always filled with a word of encouragement. This past year a letter accompanied the card. He wrote, "Jim, I am now ninety-two years old, and I may not be on this earth much longer. I have made arrangements with my family that I be buried back in Kansas. I would like for you to preside at my funeral. I hope you will do me that honor." With tears I handed it to my wife, headed upstairs and wrote a letter to Leonard, saying, "My dear teacher, it would be an honor for me to celebrate your entrance into glory." God gave me a great gift in Leonard and Katherine Deets, a gift that keeps on giving.

The classroom is a great place to learn, but God's preferred method of teaching is one on one. We learn best when people more mature in the faith take us "under their wing" and invest their time and wisdom into us. We worry far too much about credentials and gender when it comes to who is able to teach. We worry far too little about what matters most: has this person been in intimate fellowship with Jesus? Those are the people, like Katherine and Leonard, we must look to, to teach and admonish us with wisdom.

LIVING INTO THE TRUTH

Today, or this week, do one or both of the following exercises. First, if you have had an important mentor and teacher, let him or her know how much you appreciate them by sending them a card or letter (not an email!). Second, pray that God will bring you someone this week whom you can encourage, teach, admonish or offer your wisdom. You may not feel worthy, but remember, all of us are called to do this. The more you open yourself to being used by God in this way, and the more you exercise this gift, the more it will be enhanced.

AFFIRMATION

God has given each of us the ability and responsibility to teach and admonish one another with all wisdom. This day I will honor that blessing by being open to being taught, and to teaching, when the situation arises.

PRAYER

Gracious Abba, thank you for the teachers and mentors you have placed in my life. Help me to honor them and to thank them for their courage to teach me. And use me to help others as you see fit. Amen.

REFLECTION

What is the most challenging part of admonishing others?

28

SING

. . . and as you **sing**
psalms, hymns and spiritual songs.

COLOSSIANS 3:16 (NIV 1984)

Music is a completely gratuitous and unnecessary part of human life. It does not give us shelter or food, nor does it sustain human life; one would not die without music. And yet, music is a great blessing to human existence. God has designed us with ears that can take in sound, and when it is particularly beautiful or euphonic or rhythmic, it moves us.

Music can reach a deep place in our soul and touch us in a way nothing else can. Music gives rise to emotion. And sometimes it expresses feelings that cannot be expressed in any other way. Each time I sing the National Anthem at sporting events I think of the women and men who have given their lives for this country and nearly always get a tear in my eye. Music is an example of the grace of God—a freely given gift.

In Colossians 3:16, we read: "Let the word of Christ dwell in you richly as you teach and admonish one another with all wisdom, *and* as you sing psalms, hymns and spiritual songs with gratitude in your hearts to God" (NIV 1984). The word "and" tells us clearly that another way the word of Christ dwells in us is through song. Teaching is an important way in which the powerful truths of our faith are communicated. But equally important in the history of the church, and in the lives of its members, is music.

I am an admittedly terrible singer. I love to sing, but I am mindful of the ears of others, so I only sing when I am alone. When I am in a worship service I sing so softly only God can hear, which is an act of charity to my fellow worshipers. But when I am praying and praising God in private, I sing with all of my heart. I love all kinds of worship music and often sing praise songs such as "Lord, I Lift Your Name on High" and "Shout to the Lord," but am particularly fond of the older hymns. They form a regular part of my daily devotion. I sing hymns such as "How Great Thou Art," "Come Thou Fount," "Blessed Assurance," "Be Thou My Vision," "O For a Thousand Tongues," "It Is Well with My Soul" and, of course, "Amazing Grace."

When we sing, a beautiful thing happens in our soul: the deep, true and powerful words these hymns express become *our* words; they express what we are feeling toward God in a way that no other medium of communication can. The combination of the music and the words creates something greater than the sum of their parts. It is as if our soul takes wing. That is part of why hymns and praise songs become so personally meaningful to us.

As I write these words I am listening to an instrumental version of the hymn "Rock of Ages." I know the song well, so though no words are being sung, they are resonating in my mind and heart:

Rock of Ages, cleft for me,
let me hide myself in thee;
let the water and the blood,
from thy wounded side which flowed,
be of sin the double cure;
save from wrath and make me pure.

The word of Christ dwells richly in the lyrics of this hymn. It tells us, Jesus is our Rock, who is the same through the ages. You are safely hidden in the Rock of Jesus. He was pierced for our transgressions; his blood is a double cure that saves us from wrath and makes us pure. When we sing this hymn we enter into that rich word of truth, and it enfolds us.

My mother always loved to sing "When I Survey the Wondrous Cross," which she said was her favorite hymn. She remembered singing it as a little girl and how it moved her to a deep love for Jesus. When we encounter the love of God, what else can we do but praise God? When we discover this double cure that comes to us through the sacrificial love of God, what other response can we have than to offer gratitude? And what better means of communicating this gratitude, our responsive love to God, than in song? St. Augustine once wrote, "To sing is the work of a lover." To sing is a form of work, but the lover is not burdened by singing of his love for his beloved. And yet, quite often the singing we do in our churches is lackluster.

The challenge in corporate worship has always been to get the whole congregation to sing with enthusiasm. John Wesley, the founder of the Methodist church, actually put instructions for how to sing in the Methodist hymnal. In his "Directions for Singing," he writes, "Sing lustily and with good courage. Beware of singing as if you were half-dead, or half asleep; but lift your voice with strength. . . . Above all, sing spiritually. Have an eye to God in every word you sing. Aim at pleasing him more than yourself . . . and see that your heart is not carried away with the sound."

A year ago I attended a conference with over seven hundred people, all from different denominations and different parts of the country. I was standing in the front row when the worship leader led us in singing "All Creatures of Our God and King." The beautiful and powerful sound of people lifting their voices with strength came over me, giving me goose bumps. I will never forget that moment.

All worship is a response to God's prior act of love toward

us. We worship when we pray, we worship when we turn our thoughts to God, and we worship when we partake of the Lord's Supper. But we do it all because of what God has first done for us. We sing in response to a God who has always been singing over us:

> The LORD your God is with you,
>   he is mighty to save.
> He will take great delight in you,
>   he will quiet you with his love,
>   he will rejoice over you with *singing*. (Zephaniah 3:17
>   NIV 1984)

When the Holy Spirit gives us ears to hear, our hearts are stirred and our only genuine response is to sing our praise to the Lord.

LIVING INTO THE TRUTH

Today, or this week, try singing, whether in private or corporate worship, in the manner John Wesley suggests. No matter if they are hymns or praise songs, truly engage in singing them "lustily and with good courage." And as he suggests, pay attention to the words, with an "eye to God in every word you sing."

AFFIRMATION

God has been rejoicing over me with singing, taking great delight in me. My only response is to sing back to God, rejoicing and taking great delight in him.

PRAYER

Gracious Abba, thank you for the gift of music, for the gift of singing, and for the gifted men and women who write beautiful songs of worship and praise to you. May the ears of my heart be opened, so that I can hear your song of love for me, and may I respond by singing songs that express my love for you. Amen.

REFLECTION

What role has music played in your spiritual life?

WHATEVER

And **whatever** *you do, whether in*
word or deed, do it all in the name of the Lord Jesus,
giving thanks to God the Father through him.

COLOSSIANS 3:17 (NIV 1984)

One day in a class I was teaching, a student shared her appreciation for a scene in a movie she found very moving. She described it as a kind of spiritual experience. When she was finished, another young woman raised her hand and said to her classmate, "That movie is rated R. You are a Christian. You should not be seeing movies that are rated R."

Her statements set in motion a hearty, lively and sometimes passionate discussion about what Christians should, and should not, do. Several other activities were raised as gray areas: Should Christians eat meat? Can Christians drink alcohol or smoke? Is it permissible for Christians to use the Internet? And what about gambling? One student said his parents, who are dedicated church-goers, go to Las Vegas once a year. The most lively discussion came toward the end when a young man asked if Christians should kiss on the first date. "How far is too far?" he asked.

One of the things I love about the Bible is that it does not give us black-and-white answers to all the dilemmas we face. It does, however, provide basic guidelines. With that in mind, I refrained from weighing in on the discussion and instead let the students share their own insights. I did this for two reasons. One, I wanted them to engage in the issue so that they would learn to think for themselves. Too often students are trained to parrot back answers from their teachers, and this often prevents them from thinking on their own. And two, it allowed them to share their own ideas, which are often wise beyond their years.

At the end of class I said, "This has been a good discussion. Let's keep thinking about this. When we meet next time bring any new thoughts you have." They were clearly disappointed that I did not give them a simple answer, and they left a bit agitated.

The next day I overheard some of them talking in the cafeteria, and it was clear they were still holding their debate about what is, and is not, acceptable behavior for Christ-followers. When we met the following day the discussion resumed. This time they were less animated and more thoughtful. Finally, the young woman who had spoken against Christians seeing R-rated movies said, "I have done a lot of thinking, and I think I may have changed my mind."

We were all surprised by this, because she had been so vehement in her previous viewpoint. So I asked, "What happened in the last two days?"

She said, "Well, ironically, I started thinking about a movie I had seen called *Footloose*. By the way, it is rated PG!" and we all laughed. "Anyway, in that movie, a conservative Christian town has outlawed dancing. And it only made the kids want to dance more. In the end, they discovered that not all dancing is bad or leads to sin. So I thought, maybe making rules, and making everything black and white, is not the answer."

Then the student whom she had criticized for seeing an R-rated movie said, "I may have changed my mind as well." This, too, surprised us. She went on, "I got to thinking that maybe not everything I watch is good for me. I started to think about how what we put in our minds stays there and that there are a lot things that are just not good for me. I mean, the reason they rate movies is because we all agree that there are things kids shouldn't see, and if kids shouldn't see it, then why should I?" The tone of angry debate that dominated on Tuesday had dissipated on Thursday. Again, I stayed silent. More students shared their thoughts, and each one brought about a new and valuable insight.

Finally, one student said, "Okay, Jim, you have stayed out of this long enough. What do you think about this?"

I said, "First, I think the way you have gone about this issue is brilliant. The Bible leaves a lot of questions unanswered, which allows us to think, under the leading of the Spirit. Second, though we do not have clear, easy answers to these kinds of questions, we do have one basic guideline. Paul said to the Corinthians, 'So whether you eat or drink or whatever you do, do it all for the glory of God' (1 Corinthians 10:31). Instead of asking, 'Can Christians _____ (gamble, dance, drink wine)?' the better question is, 'Can I do this in the name of Jesus and for his glory?' Our lives as Christ-followers are completely immersed in Jesus. We died and rose with him and he lives in us. Our ethics must be tied to our identity."

Another student spoke up: "I think I get what you are saying. Since Christ lives in me, and since he is my life, the question is not about what is right and what is wrong, the question is, does this glorify God?" I nodded in agreement. Then he went on, "So, how do you know? How do you know if it glorifies God or if you can give thanks for it or if you can do it in the name of Jesus?" It was a good question.

"All I can say," I answered, "is that I try to listen to the Spirit. When I feel uneasy about something—a movie, a discussion, an activity—I try to discern whether or not the Spirit is telling me it's not good. If I sense it's not, I simply stop. One time I watched a great TV show—well acted, Emmy nominated but very dark in its content. I never felt good after watching it, so I prayed, and the Spirit gently let me know that it was not good for me. So I stopped watching it.

"But," I went on to say, "this principle is not only to help us know what not to do; it also tells us about how to go about doing all that we do. Paul told the Colossians, '*whatever* you do, whether in word or deed, do it all in the name of the Lord Jesus, giving thanks to God the Father through him' (Colossians 3:17). Notice that word: *whatever.* Everything that we do—every word and every action—is to be done in Jesus' name, and with thanksgiving. It's not just about what we don't do; it's about how we go about living every second of every day. Every moment is a gift, every breath is a gift, everything we eat and drink is a gift. In a sense, all of life is a sacrament, a sacred gift from God. Whatever we do, we do for his glory, because we are his, and he is our life."

Easy answers make life easier, but God's main aim in our lives is not merely to get us to do the right things and to stop doing the wrong things. His aim is to teach us how to love him, to love life, and to do all that we do with him and for his glory. The activity is not so much what's in question as the heart of the person who does it. Rules do not shape our hearts. They make us focus on the activity rather than the condition of our hearts. Living under the leading of the Holy Spirit is what shapes us into new people, people who live for God and glorify him in all they do. That is God's great divine plan—in "whatever" we do.

LIVING INTO THE TRUTH

Today, or this week, take a moment to ask the Spirit to reveal any area or activity in your life that may not glorify God. See if there is anything that you engage in that would be difficult for you to do while giving thanks to God at the same time. Let the Spirit search your heart as you ponder whether or not this activity can be done in Jesus' name.

AFFIRMATION

All things are lawful for me, but not all things are beneficial and not all things glorify God. Whatever I do—what I say and what I engage in—can and should be done in Jesus' name and for his glory.

PRAYER

Gracious Abba, I have come to see that not everything in life is black and white. Help me to discern what is good and beneficial for me and what is not. Lead me, Holy Spirit, into a life that constantly glorifies you. In Jesus' name, amen.

REFLECTION

What is one area that you would like to see become an activity you could do for God's glory?

- 30 -

NAME

And whatever you do, whether in
word or deed, do it all in the **name** *of the Lord Jesus,*
giving thanks to God the Father through him.

COLOSSIANS 3:17 (NIV 1984)

Nearly every time Christians end their prayers they say, "In Jesus' name, amen." What does it mean to pray "in Jesus' *name*"? When we baptize people, why does the minister say, "In the *name* of the Father, the Son and the Holy Spirit," as they dunk or douse the initiate?

For many years I had absolutely no understanding of what it actually meant to pray in Jesus' name. I just said it ("In Jesus' name, amen) in the same way I might say, "Roger—over and out" when talking on a walkie-talkie. I assumed it was just the way you ended prayers. While I'm sure that God did not reject my prayers even though I had no idea what the ending meant, I certainly had much to learn. Thankfully, I discovered why we pray (and baptize and minister) in Jesus' name. And it has made a great difference.

To act in the name of another means to act on their behalf, to operate with the authority of that person. It means to proceed as if that person were present with you and to perform that action as if that person were doing it himself or herself. Ambassadors, for example, go forth with the authority and power of the person or country they represent. So when the Secretary of State of the United States goes to another country, she not only speaks for her country but acts with the full authority and power of the United States. Likewise, when we pray or minister or parent in the name of Jesus, we are doing this action with the authority, presence and power of Jesus himself.

The authority, presence and power of Jesus is another way to describe the kingdom of God, where God rules and reigns. It is strong and unshakeable. We align our little kingdoms and queendoms with the kingdom of God when we choose to live as apprentices of Jesus, our teacher and master, doing the things he called us to do. As we do that, we act with his power. Jesus' first disciples learned this when they began to minister in Jesus' name after his ascension. One of my favorite verses is Acts 8:12, where Philip has been extending the kingdom of God in Samaria:

> But when they believed Philip as he proclaimed the good news of *the kingdom of God and the name of Jesus Christ,* they were baptized, both men and women.

Notice the combination: "the kingdom of God and the name of Jesus Christ." The kingdom of God was not a nice idea to these disciples; it was a reality they relied on. And they accessed that reality through the name of Jesus. Philip was not acting out of his own strength; he was working and accomplishing all he did with the strength of Jesus and the power of his kingdom. In doing what they did "in Jesus' name," in a very real sense Jesus was still acting—not independently, but with them.

We are all called to "grow in grace" (see 2 Peter 3:18). We do this not by sinning more and needing more forgiveness but by accessing God's grace—his power and presence and resources—when we act in Jesus' name. God's intention for all of us is that we might get to the place where more and more of our daily actions are assisted by grace. I used to think that only sinners needed grace, but now I see that sinners need very little grace, because they are not acting in Jesus' name. The great saints consumed an enormous amount of grace. They relied on God in every dimension of their lives. As Dallas Willard has often said, "Saints burn grace like 747's burn jet fuel."

The main ideas behind this book can be summed up in two powerful truths that describe who we are and where we live:

First, "I am (your name) in whom Christ dwells." Second, "I live in the strong and unshakeable kingdom of God." These are not make-believe, wishful ideas or positive thoughts. They describe reality. Jesus is with you. Your life is safe and secure, hidden in God. Your destiny is not up for grabs. You will one day be revealed with Jesus in glory. You—who Jesus said are the light of the world—are one day going to radiate as bright as the sun. Because of who you are (one whom Christ has raised and made new and now dwells in), sin has no place in your life. You do not run on sin anymore. You run on grace.

So in truth there is nothing you cannot do. In this world we have troubles. Our careers do not take off or they sputter. Our relationships sometimes fall apart. Our dreams and hopes are dashed by dire circumstances. We lose loved ones, we suffer losses, and we undergo trials. People let us down. We let ourselves down. But thanks be to God, we are not managing this universe. God, through Christ, is. And by his grace we are made partakers of a new, divine nature. So we wake up and face a new day, not alone, relying only on our own resources. We awaken to each new day with God at our side, our good shepherd who walks beside us, leading us to still waters and quiet places, through dark valleys, and into great feasts. His goodness and mercy pursue us all the days of our lives.

That is what it means to do all that we do "in Jesus' *name*."

What if our entire lives became devoted to living as apprentices of Jesus, immersed in his power and presence, living each day moving step by step toward an inner transformation into the character of Christ? If we were to make that our constant aim, God would triumph in and through us, the world would be changed, and the gates of hell would rattle. Of this I am certain. After all, Jesus gathered a group of rag-tag individuals two thousand years ago and taught them how to live in his presence with his power. And he did it with only twelve. The world is hungering for such people. Will you join me?

LIVING INTO THE TRUTH

Today, or this week, take on a new project (through action or prayer) with the clear intention of engaging in it in the name of Jesus. Remember, this means to act with the presence and power of Jesus, and also in the manner of Jesus. Intentionally train yourself to act *with* Jesus, not merely on his behalf. Utilize as much grace as you can, stepping out more and more in confidence, knowing that God is with you and working through you.

AFFIRMATION

I am privileged to act, to pray, to minister and to do all that I do in Jesus' name. I do not act alone; I operate with the power and presence of Jesus in all that I do.

PRAYER

Gracious Abba, thank you for allowing me to act in your name. I did nothing to deserve this incredible gift. Help me to do all that I do in the spirit that regards you as my all in all. Help me to co-labor with you this day, as together we advance your kingdom. Amen.

REFLECTION

What thoughts or feelings did you have about ending a prayer in "Jesus' name" before reading this chapter?

How might the teaching of this chapter shift what that means to you?

GROUP DISCUSSION GUIDE

The discussion guide covers six-chapter groupings, allowing you to cover the book in five sessions. These sessions are designed to fill about an hour-long discussion. Some of the questions in the group guide are also found at the end of the chapters, and some are new. This will allow you to summarize what you have learned with your group.

Covering just six of the chapters each week gives space for group members to miss a day of study each week or to take more than one day on each chapter. If you want to cover the book in smaller or larger portions, feel free to find the pace that is right for your group. You may, for example, want to have a group discussion every two weeks in order to allow plenty of time to read the chapters and to "live into the truth" by practicing each exercise.

It is important to establish your group as a place of open

and supportive conversation. Don't judge each other if you aren't able to finish all of the material each week. And be aware that you will respond in different ways to the exercises. Some group members may find some of the exercises more comfortable and nurturing than others. Talk about this openly.

If you want to challenge each other to memorize the passage, you might want to recite the verses covered each week together rather than simply reading them from your Bible.

SESSION ONE: CHAPTERS ONE TO SIX

OPEN

- Discuss your experiences with the "living into the truth" exercises.

  Chapter 1: the empty tomb

  Chapter 2: practicing the presence

  Chapter 3: two truths

  Chapter 4: things of the Spirit

  Chapter 5: memory verse

  Chapter 6: saying grace

READ OR RECITE

- Have someone read aloud the verses of Colossians that were covered in these chapters: Colossians 3:1-4.

Discuss

Chapter 1: Raised

- Have you known, and been living your Christian life from, this reality (that you died and rose with Jesus)? If not, why do you suppose it was never explained to you?

- What difference can this insight have in your life as an apprentice of Jesus?

- What impact might this reality have on a group of Christians, either as a church community or as a fellowship group?

Chapter 2: With

- What does life look and feel like when you are aware that God is with you? What difference does it make?

Chapter 3: Seated

- What is the relationship between how God forgives and how we forgive one another?

Chapter 4: Set

- Why do you think it is so difficult to keep our minds set on the things of God and not on the things of this earth?

- If you could only set your mind on one truth of God (mentioned above), what would it be? Why?

Chapter 5: Hidden

- What part or parts of your life are hidden with Christ?
- When is it difficult for you to believe that God delights in you? Why do you think this is the case?

Chapter 6: Life

- Why is it impossible to be alive spiritually and disconnected from Jesus?
- What are the most spiritually nourishing practices for you? Why are they so helpful to you?

CLOSE

- Wrap up your time together with the hymn quoted in chapter one, "Give Me Jesus." Play a CD or YouTube version, or sing it together if you are so inclined.

SESSION TWO: CHAPTERS SEVEN TO TWELVE

OPEN

- Discuss your experiences with the "living into the truth" exercises.
  Chapter 7: act of kindness
  Chapter 8: consecrated to God
  Chapter 9: shut the door to sin
  Chapter 10: new habits for our bodies

Chapter 11: expose your heart to God

Chapter 12: sin and consequence

READ OR RECITE

- Have someone read aloud the verses of Colossians that were covered in these chapters: Colossians 3:4-6.

DISCUSS

Chapter 7: Revealed

- Have you ever accidentally found something out (e.g., the outcome of a game) before others did and had to hold your tongue to keep them in suspense? How did that feel?

- How can knowing that, in the end, we will be with Jesus in glory affect how you live the days of your life until then?

Chapter 8: You

- What is the usual way we try to stop sinning, and why does it fail?

Chapter 9: Mortify

- How does understanding the sacredness of who we are help us put away sin? Why do you think God has arranged for us to continue to have to struggle with sin even after we have become "people in whom Christ dwells"?

- How would you describe your own journey with seeing sin for what it really is (that which is destructive)? Are you there yet?

Chapter 10: Bodies

- Why is it often hard for us to make a connection between our bodies and our spirits?
- What are some ways you can begin training your body to become your ally in your spiritual journey?

Chapter 11: Desires

- What does our culture teach us about desire and moderation?
- How does intimacy with God reorder our desires?

Chapter 12: Wrath

- Have you ever found it hard to reconcile the love of God and the wrath of God? Explain.
- What do you think about Dallas Willard's point that it is not that we are "sinners in the hands of an angry God," but that God has fallen into the hands of angry sinners who project this false narrative of wrath onto God?

CLOSE

- Wrap up your time together with the hymn quoted in

chapter eight, "Take My Life" by Francis Havergal. Play a CD or YouTube version, or sing it together if you are so inclined.

SESSION THREE: CHAPTERS THIRTEEN TO EIGHTEEN

OPEN

- Discuss your experiences with the "living into the truth" exercises.
  Chapter 13: reflect on light, truth, love
  Chapter 14: live as an apprentice
  Chapter 15: say ten kind things
  Chapter 16: putting on virtues
  Chapter 17: read John 5
  Chapter 18: reach out to someone different

READ OR RECITE

- Have someone read aloud the verses of Colossians that were covered in these chapters: Colossians 3:7-11.

DISCUSS

Chapter 13: Walk

- Have you ever seen someone from a distance and known who it was just by his or her walk or posture?

- Which of the three gifts that we are called to walk in (light, truth, love) would you like to see more of in your life? How does this gift speak to you?

Chapter 14: Once

- "Cradle Christian" is a term to describe people who grew up in the church and always considered them-selves as a Christian. On the other hand, "convert Christian" describes people who remember a time when they were not a Christian. Are you a cradle or a convert Christian? How does that influence this issue of who you *once* were and who you are now?

- Why is it so tempting to focus on external behavior and not internal identity?

Chapter 15: Mouth

- Have you ever been the victim of abusive words? How did it feel?

- Why does anger enlist the lips to carry out its desire to hurt?

- What are some ways you can begin to train your tongue to be a blessing?

Chapter 16: Clothes

- Of the five virtues, which one is the most comfortable for you to wear?

- Of the five virtues, which is the most challenging for you to put on?

Chapter 17: Knowledge

- Do you agree that knowledge is power? How have you seen this reality in your life?

- The role of the Spirit is to reveal the true nature of the Father and the Son and their self-sacrificial love. Do you think most Christians really know this? Why or why not?

Chapter 18: All

- Have you ever witnessed an example of true unity in diversity, such as that of Perpetua and Felicitas?

- Why is it so challenging, even today, for Christians to overcome our differences and live together in this unity in diversity?

CLOSE

- Use the text in chapter sixteen to pray for each other to be clothed in the five virtues. Pray through the following commitment liturgy. After each line allow a time of silence for people to pray more specifically around each virtue.

  #### A Prayer for Virtue

  I resolve to set aside judgment and gently slip on *compassion* for the people I meet today.

  [Silence]

I will show *kindness* today. I will try to open doors for people, let them in my lane while driving, smile at people and speak encouraging words.

[Silence]

I resolve to put on *humility* this day by not thinking highly of myself and instead thinking highly of others.

[Silence]

I will not use strength this day to be aggressive, but rather, I will use my strength to be *gentle* on this day.

[Silence]

Today I will remember who I am and who is in control. I resolve to put on *patience* this day and simply let things be as they are.

[Silence]

Amen.

SESSION FOUR: Chapters Nineteen to Twenty-Four

Open

- Discuss your experiences with the "living into the truth" exercises.

Chapter 19: grasping God's love
Chapter 20: listen to the Spirit
Chapter 21: pray for someone
Chapter 22: pray for grace to forgive
Chapter 23: read Philippians 2:5-11
Chapter 24: the peace of Christ

READ OR RECITE

- Have someone read aloud the verses of Colossians that were covered in these chapters: Colossians 3:12-15.

DISCUSS

Chapter 19: Chosen

- Have you ever felt that particular inner feeling that God truly loves you and has chosen you? Describe.
- What is the relationship between being declared holy by God, and walking in holiness in terms of our behavior?

Chapter 20: Beloved

- If you could really and truly believe that you are loved without condition, how would it change your behavior?

Chapter 21: Bear

- The chapter says, "Bearing with one another is the only way to love and be loved." Do you agree or disagree? Explain.

- Why is bearing with each other seen as an obligation and not as an opportunity?

Chapter 22: Forgive

- What do you think about the notion that pride is the primary barrier that prevents us from forgiving others?
- How do you understand the idea that forgiveness is not about justice, it's about healing? Has this been true for you in the past? Explain.

Chapter 23: Love

- This chapter says that order is important in love. Do you agree? Why or why not?
- While our culture loves love, it does not know how to love. How have you seen this to be true?

Chapter 24: Peace

- Why does simply "giving peace a chance" not succeed?
- Have you been a part of a group that was good at handling disagreement? What was that like?

CLOSE

- God is smiling at you. As a group sit in quiet for a few minutes with that truth, picturing yourself being showered with God's pleasure. Close with prayers of thanksgiving.

SESSION FIVE: CHAPTERS TWENTY-FIVE TO THIRTY

OPEN

- Discuss your experiences with the "living into the truth" exercises.

  Chapter 25: gratitude journal

  Chapter 26: meditate on Luke 1:26-38

  Chapter 27: thank a mentor, be a mentor

  Chapter 28: sing your worship

  Chapter 29: glorify God

  Chapter 30: act in the name of Jesus

READ OR RECITE

- Have someone read aloud the verses of Colossians that were covered in these chapters: Colossians 3:15-17.

DISCUSS

Chapter 25: Thankful

- Why is it easy to overlook the gratuitous nature of life, to begin to assume we deserve the good things we have in life?

- How does understanding the provision of God's abundant kingdom lead us naturally to give thanks?

Chapter 26: Word

- Have you ever felt like the Bible was dry and hard to understand?

- What are the primary conditions needed to hear the word of Christ?

Chapter 27: Teach

- Who are your most significant teachers?
- How do you feel about the call to teach others?

Chapter 28: Sing

- What role has music played in your spiritual life?
- What is your favorite hymn or praise song? What about that song has been meaningful to you?

Chapter 29: Whatever

- What activity have you wondered about being acceptable for Christ-followers to engage in? Why?
- The teaching in this chapter is that it is important to live into the questions and to listen to the Spirit. Why is this so much more challenging than having simple, black-and-white answers?

Chapter 30: Name

- What, if anything, in this chapter was a new idea for you?
- Do you agree that a small gathering of people whose only aim is to do all that they do in the presence, power

and manner of Jesus could change the world? If so, why does it so often fail to come to pass?

- What next steps would you like to take in your own Christian life in light of what you have learned from Colossians 3 over the past few weeks?

CLOSE

- Ahead of time ask group members to suggest a favorite hymn or praise song. Play them via audio or video, or sing some of them together to close your session.

Notes

p. 51   "The New Testament never speaks": James S. Stewart, *Walking with God* (Vancouver, BC: Regent College Publishing, 1996), p. 19.

p. 73   "Biological evidence suggests": Meredith B. McGuire, "Why Bodies Matter: A Sociological Reflection in Spirituality and Materiality," in *Minding the Spirit: The Study of Christian Spirituality*, ed. Elizabeth A. Dreyer and Mark S. Burrows (Baltimore: Johns Hopkins University Press, 2005), p. 120.

p. 81   "The more our desires are directed": James Houston, *The Heart's Desire* (Colorado Springs: NavPress, 1996).

p. 85   "inevitable consequences": F. F. Bruce, *The Epistle to the Colossians, to Philemon, and to the Ephesians*, New International Commentary on the New Testament (Grand Rapids: Eerdmans, 1984), p. 144.

p. 85   "conscience and constitution": Ibid.

p. 90   "participation in a course of life": T. K. Abbott, *A Critical and Exegetical Commentary on the Epistles to the Ephesians and to the Colossians,* The International Critical Commentary, ed. S. R. Driver, A. Plummer and C. A. Briggs (Edinburgh, Scotland: T & T Clark, 2000), p. 282.

p. 122   "Humanity is a word which you look for": Ibid., p. 285.

p. 123   "See how they love one another": Tertullian, *Apology* 39.7.

p. 132   "After a mother has smiled at her child": Hans Urs von Balthasar, *Love Alone Is Credible*, trans. D. C. Schindler (San Francisco: Ignatius Press, 2004), p. 76.

p. 134   "God has already seen in him": Ibid., p. 103.

p. 139   "My friends ain't the way": Used by permission.

p. 152   catching love: This idea of "catching love" comes from Dallas Willard, *The Divine Conspiracy: Rediscovering Our Hidden Life in God* (San Francisco: HarperCollins, 1998), p. 183.

p. 158   "the peace which belongs to His kingdom": Abbott, *Ephesians and Colossians*, p. 289.

p. 158   "Where there is a conflict of motives or desires": Lightfoot, *Colossians and Philemon*, p. 112.

p. 182   "Sing lustily and with good courage": *The United Methodist Hymnal* (Nashville: United Methodist Publishing House, 1989), p. vii.

God is stamping "aprentis" hearts with his kingdom purposes.
He'll use *you* to change the world.

APRENTIS SERVES

Churches. Through a ministry of discipleship and formation, God can radically transform the way your church community lives and works and loves.

Like-minded leaders, organizations and thinkers. Collaborate with us to archive, engage and expand the field of Christian spiritual formation.

Students. Through an undergraduate degree track and second major in Christian spiritual formation, you can begin a serious life transformation through your college experience.

*Begin an "**apprentice**" journey today.*
For more information, contact the Aprentis Institute
at 316.295.5519 or email Aprentis@friends.edu.

APRENTIS
Institute for Christian Spiritual Formation

FRIENDS
UNIVERSITY

THE
APPRENTICE
SERIES

The Good and Beautiful God

The Good and Beautiful Life

The Good and Beautiful Community

For more information and resources visit
www.apprenticeofJesus.org